The ULTIMATE GUIDE *to a*
48 HOUR BOOK

Everything you need to know about preparing your book and ordering from the fastest book printer in the world!

JIM FULTON

The Ultimate Guide to a 48 Hour Book
Copyright © 2018 by Jim Fulton

ISBN: 978-1-948791-00-7 (pb)

Seventh Edition (2021)

Printed in United States of America by 48 Hour Books
www.48HrBooks.com

About this book: The cover of this book showcases our 10pt C1S cover with a Silk Laminate coating. The front cover features Diamond 3D Clear on the title and on our logo. It also features Diamond 3D Foil (in gold) on the words "48 Hour Book." The inside pages are printed on our standard 60# bright white offset paper. The main body font is Garamond 12pt, and the heading font is Nunito Light, 36pt.

Table of Contents

1

chapter one

What This Book
Is About

SAMPLE: 10pt C1S Cover
with Gloss UV Coating
(our standard cover)

> *"Our life is frittered away by detail...simplify, simplify."*
>
> —Henry David Thoreau

While these are great words of wisdom, they shouldn't be applied universally. The contractor who built your house, for example, had better have been paying attention to the details. Likewise with an author writing a book and getting it printed. There are dozens of details to be aware of, and you better stay on top of each one of them.

At 48 Hour Books, we believe that a well-informed author is our best client. This book seeks to simplify the sometimes daunting task of getting your book into print. We take those dozens of details, break them down into an easily understood sequence of choices, explain each one thoroughly, and even make recommendations that can save you time and money.

Don't feel as though you have to read the entire book from beginning to end. While it's a pretty easy read, you can certainly save some time by skipping a chapter here and there if the subject matter isn't something that concerns you.

Here is a breakdown of each chapter, to help guide your reading priorities.

CHAPTERS TWO AND THREE explain a little bit about who we are, what sets us apart from other book printers out there, and what our philosophy is. I think you'll find it refreshing.

CHAPTER FOUR touches on Amazon, and suggestions for selling your book through alternative methods instead.

CHAPTER FIVE goes into detail about our Free Book Templates ... where to get them, how to use them, and our recommended "best practices" when writing your book. While these recommendations are specific to Microsoft Word, they can be adapted to virtually any word processing program. We then list several sources available for additional help and training in Microsoft Word, or other common word processing programs like Word Perfect, Pages, or Open Office.

CHAPTERS SIX AND SEVEN start to get into the real meat of the matter. Here, we'll discuss some of the choices you'll have to make when formatting your book. We compare 'formatting' with 'editing,' which are completely different, and not understanding those differences can be an expensive mistake.

CHAPTER EIGHT describes how to create a 'print-ready' PDF file from your Word document. It's really pretty easy, and if you do it right, it will save you money. Of course, if you'd rather just have us do the formatting for you, we're happy to help.

CHAPTER NINE takes you through placing an order online. It breaks down each step involved, the options available, and the cost of each option.

CHAPTERS TEN AND ELEVEN break down exactly what happens to your order. A simplified flowchart helps describe each step of the process. You'll see how easy it is to keep track of your order online as it goes from formatting and layout, to printing, binding, and shipping.

CHAPTER TWELVE lists just some of our FAQs.

CHAPTER THIRTEEN details our Terms and Conditions of Sale. Yes, it's a lot of legaleze, and frankly, people rarely read the Terms and Conditions of Sale anymore, but we've emphasized a few of the important items, and encourage you to at least read these bolded parts. As we said, an informed author is our best client.

CHAPTER FOURTEEN touches briefly on recycling.

CHAPTER FIFTEEN contains samples of our paper options, with plenty of photography to better illustrate the differences. Use this section when choosing your interior paper. We also include samples of most of our cover materials, but they're not in this chapter. Rather, they are scattered throughout the book as chapter dividers. You'll not only be able to feel the difference between 10 pt. and 12 pt., but also the difference between Silk Laminate, Gloss Laminate, and UV Coating.

"During the process of getting my book ready for print, I had many questions and was able to call and immediately speak to a knowledgeable individual to get help. It seems the norm today is to call a company and go through an endless array of menu options that lead nowhere, but 48 Hour Books is one of the few exceptions."

- Chuck R.

2

chapter two

What Sets 48 Hour Books Apart from Others?

Three simple words: Speed, Help, ~~Quality~~

We ♥ books!

"There are other things that set us apart from the competition, but the three most obvious are our speed, the help we offer, and our quality."

Speed

Just how fast are we? For example, all of our standard, everyday perfect bound book orders have a 2 day production time. We also have Rush service available, which speeds production up by 1 day, as well as Super Rush, which speeds production up by 2 days—meaning your books could ship the same day you order!

We are incredibly efficient. We have to be, because we're printing and shipping thousands of books every day, and we *always* meet our deadlines. So whether our authors have a book signing, a seminar, or a family reunion, they know they'll get their books on time, every time.

This sense of urgency extends to every aspect of our business, from answering your questions, to giving you a quote, to sending you proofs. After all, what good is incredibly fast production if it takes several weeks just to get your first PDF Proof?

Not in a hurry? No problem! You can take as long as you need to review proofs—we won't rush you through the process.

Speed Before You Even Place an Order

If you've got questions, we encourage you to call us (800-231-0521), email us (info@48hrbooks.com), or use our online chat system. We answer our phones and reply quickly to emails.

The other guys often take 2 days or more just to return an email. There have been many times when we've answered a question, gotten the order, and printed and shipped the full order, all before our competitors have even answered the initial question! Our new clients delight in telling our competitors, *"Well, thanks ... but I already got my books, and they look beautiful."*

Speed Creating Your Proofs

Most PDF Proofs are available within a few hours, and only about one in five orders take more than a day for the PDF Proof. So, if you send us files in the morning, you'll probably get a PDF Proof that afternoon. But every order is different, and some will take longer than others—especially reformatting jobs. It's always best to send us your files as soon as you can, and we'll get your PDF Proof back to you as quickly as possible. When we get your files, we immediately get to work. The other guys might take a week or two. If you come back with changes, we can generally send a revised proof within hours. The other guys might be another week or so. You can see how this alone can make a huge difference in the turn-around time of your full order.

Help...As in Exceptional Customer Service

First of all, we answer our phones. That alone sets us apart from almost all of our competition. We like to hear from you, and we want to make sure that you're aware of what's happening with your order and that you understand and are happy with the options that you've chosen. If you have a question about anything book-related, we encourage you to call or email us. We also have online chat available, if you'd rather communicate that way. So between phone calls (immediate), online chat (immediate), and email (normally returned within minutes), we've got you covered.

You'll be assigned your own Customer Service Rep from our great Customer Service team. He or she will be there to guide you through the entire process, whenever you need help.

If you have a particular date by which you need your books, let us know. We'll work with you to determine exactly when you'll need to approve your Proofs in order to get your books on time. We'll do whatever we can to keep you on schedule. If you fall behind schedule, we'll work with you to find the most efficient way to revise your order so you get your books on time.

We're very flexible. If your book has something a little out-of-the-ordinary, we can usually work with you to make it happen.

Our Customer Service Team is available Monday thru Friday, from 8:30am to 5:00pm EST, but we often have a couple of people staying later, or coming in earlier, so you're welcome to try us after hours, too. How's that for flexibility?

Some of our larger competitors brag about producing books without human interaction. We have state-of-the-art equipment, but we still count on several sets of eyes checking your order every step of the way. While we don't have the time to read your entire book (we're printing, binding and shipping within 48 hours, remember), if we do happen to see something that we think may not be right, we'll contact you immediately. This alone has saved authors tens of thousands of dollars over the years. It's just another indication of how we work for you, and try to give you the best product possible.

Quality...
Bookstore Quality

We start with state-of-the-art digital presses. Our black-and-white presses are the fastest available, and their registration and repeatability are unmatched. Our color presses produce near photo-quality color images, which are great for photo books and high school yearbooks. We use these same high-quality presses for all of our color work, so even the small pictures in cookbooks, memoirs, and family histories still look great. Consistency is very important to us. You shouldn't be able to pull out three books from your order and see three different shades of blue on the cover. With orders from 48 Hour Books, you'll see that from the first book to the last, they'll all be consistently beautiful.

Our paper is a little more expensive than most, but it can make a big difference in the look and feel of your finished book. And, because we order our paper by the truckload, our paper costs aren't much higher than the cheap paper that some competitors use. Our standard book paper is a 60# bright white opaque sheet that's a little heavier than what most of the competition uses. It's considered a #1 sheet, so it's a high-quality sheet. Its surface is smooth and consistent from sheet to sheet. Because it's a bright white, the contrast between paper and the printed word is enhanced, so it's easier to read. And, since it's opaque, there's not as much show-through from the back side of the sheet. We also offer the same paper in heavier weights of 70# and 80#, each progressively thicker, heavier, and more opaque. Additionally, we offer a cream offset paper for a softer look, in both 60# and 70#. We also have coated papers: You'll have a choice of a satiny, Silk paper, or a Gloss paper, each available in either 80# or 100# text. And just like with our uncoated papers, these are high quality sheets, not cut-rate factory seconds. The difference may not always be obvious, but a high-quality sheet is the necessary starting point for a high-quality book.

The most obvious difference in quality is in our bindery department. We use state-of-the-art perfect binders, and the right adhesive.

In book binding, there are two types of adhesive that are used around the world: EVA (Ethylene Vinyl Acetate) and PUR (Polyurethane Reactive). EVA adhesive is quick, easy, and fairly inexpensive. However, it doesn't hold up very well in extreme temperatures (like the back of a UPS truck that might hit 140° in the summertime, or -10° in the winter time). If EVA gets too hot, it melts. If it gets too cold, it gets brittle. Either way, the pages start to fall out. PUR requires specialized equipment, needs more daily maintenance, takes longer to dry, and is more expensive. With PUR, the end product is so much better (not only better looking, but also significantly more durable), that several years ago, we made the decision to change our entire operation over to PUR adhesive. It was a massive, and very expensive changeover, but it's been worth it. Today, our books are actually better than "bookstore quality," because I've seen plenty of books in bookstores that use the old EVA adhesive.

We also use a double-hinge score on our covers. This not only provides for a nice square spine edge, but also takes some pressure off of the spine when readers open their books. It's a small touch, but it's made a big difference in the quality of our books. Here again, I've seen a fair number of books at bookstores that don't have this hinge score at the spine, so those books just aren't going to hold up as well.

In addition to the Big Three (Speed, Help, and Quality), we provide many other benefits that none of our competitors can match. Sure, a few of them may offer one or two of the following, but only 48 Hour Books offers all of these:

Hard Cover Books & Dust Jackets

Offer your readers a premium version of your book, suitable for display as a 'coffee table' book. We can print your full order as hard cover books, or do a combination of some perfect bound and some hard cover ... it's up to you.

When walking down the New Releases aisle of your local bookstore or library, you may notice something -- all of the hard cover (also

Indigo blue Pearl Linen cover with a Silk Laminate Dust Jacket

known as "case bound") books have a dust jacket, a removable laminated cover that wraps around the existing cover of the book. With 48 Hour Books, your case bound books can have beautifully-printed, full-color dust jackets to give the book a really polished look!

In addition to providing protection to the cover of your book, our dust jackets include two 3.5 inch flaps that wrap inside the book, allowing for additional printing space. This space can be used for any number of things, such as a book summary or an About the Author section.

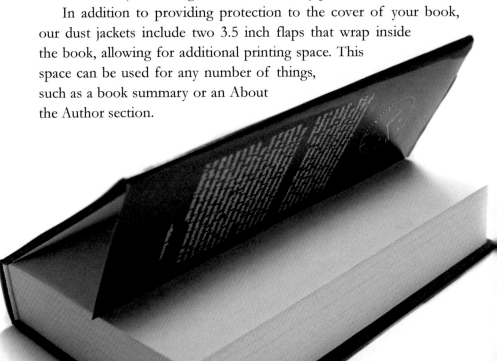

Cloth and Leather Covers

Another unique premium selection that can give your books a rich, elegant look is our different cloth and leather choices. While the Leather and the Pearl Linen cloth covers are intended for hard cover books, we also offer a leatherette cover for perfect bound, coil bound, and saddle-stitched books.

Forest green Leather cover with gold Foil Stamping

Foil Stamping

We can add foil stamping to cloth or leather covers, another way to help your book really stand out from the crowd. Our new (raised!) Diamond 3D Foil is available for other cover types.

Diamond 3D Covers

Your book cover may be the most important aspect of marketing your book. No matter how much effort you spend getting people to your book signing or to your book's web page, they won't buy the book if the cover isn't enticing.

Book stores display books with their covers facing the reader. It's the first thing they'll see, and an eye-catching cover is the reason they'll pick up a book. No longer just considered 'nice to have', a professionally designed cover is now an essential part of marketing your book.

As an author, you've only got a few seconds to convince them that your book might be worth a longer look. You may have some great comments and reviews on your back cover, but you have to have a front cover that's enticing enough for a reader to pick it up and actually read the back.

Highlight elements of your design with Diamond 3D Clear!

Exclusively from 48 Hour Books, **Diamond 3D Covers** are an inexpensive way to really make your book covers stand out from the crowd. We'll highlight a couple of elements on your cover with our exclusive Diamond 3D printing, which gives you the look (and feel) of a best-seller at a fraction of the cost. This means you'll be able to catch your readers' attention by including metallic foil on the cover of your book without breaking the bank!

We now offer Diamond 3D in three options: Foil, Clear, and Smart Textures. Check out pages 72-73 for some more information about these exciting new options!

Photos don't do these justice: The front cover of this book—The Ultimate Guide to a 48 Hour Book—is a good sample of both our Diamond 3D Clear and our Diamond 3D Foil options).

Gold Diamond 3D Foil really catches the eye!

Reformatting Like the Best Sellers

Choose from a variety of best-sellers, and we'll format your book to match their formatting. Why re-invent the wheel? If it worked for these best-selling authors, it can work for you, too.

Create-a-Cover

A simple way to get a great looking, high-quality cover at a fraction of the cost of a custom cover design.

Help Promoting Your Book

Want some free exposure for your books? We advertise like crazy, both in print and online, and we occasionally use images of books that we've printed. If you'd like us to use your books in our advertising, simply let us know!

We also send out an e-mail newsletter on a regular basis and we love to feature authors of books we've recently printed! Contact us if you'd like to sign up to receive our newsletter or if you'd like the chance to be featured in our "Spotlight" section: email our marketing department at: sm@48HrBooks.com

3

chapter three

No Contracts...

You keep all rights and all profits

We're Not Vanity Publishers. We Are Strictly Book Printers.

Vanity publishers can be very cunning. They will try to sell you their "Silver" or "Gold" package, which may cost thousands of dollars up front. They'll talk about putting your book on their website, maybe even in a featured position on their home page, and making it available to bookstores. They'll promise you "high royalties," which might be 10%-15% of the sales price. You can almost see the cash registers ringing with sales already, right? But once you've signed their contract, they'll take your manuscript, take your money and maybe, just maybe, they'll print a few copies of your book (usually poor quality). They won't consult you and they won't offer any help with the marketing or distribution of your book. Vanity publishers have no relationships with bookshops. In fact, many bookshops plain refuse to stock the books they produce. They may make it available on their website, but frankly, their site doesn't get enough web traffic to make any significant sales, and a 15% royalty of zero sales is still zero. They really aren't interested in selling copies of your book, since they've already made their profit from that hefty "Gold package" fee they already charged you.

So, more often than not, the author ends up several thousand dollars down with a small handful of books that they cannot sell. That's vastly different from the way 48 Hour Books operates.

We are strictly book printers. We don't have contracts to sign, we don't sell your books, either online or through bookstores. Our authors have their own sales methods, whether through book signings, conventions, seminars, on their own website, or through Amazon. But THEY handle all of that, and they keep all of the profits. We don't claim any rights to your book, and we won't sell your books in the future.

The only thing you are paying us to do is print (and ship) your books. Even if you choose our design services, they're just one-time charges. Once you've got a cover design, you don't need it again for reprint orders. So if your book sells for $15 and it costs $4 to print and ship, the remaining $11 (73%) is all profit. That sure beats a royalty of 15% of nothing.

We work with you to design and lay out your book, make corrections for you if possible, and charge a very reasonable fee for printing. You'll get great quality books, and you'll get them much faster than anywhere else.

4

chapter four

Is Amazon the "Holy Grail" for Authors?

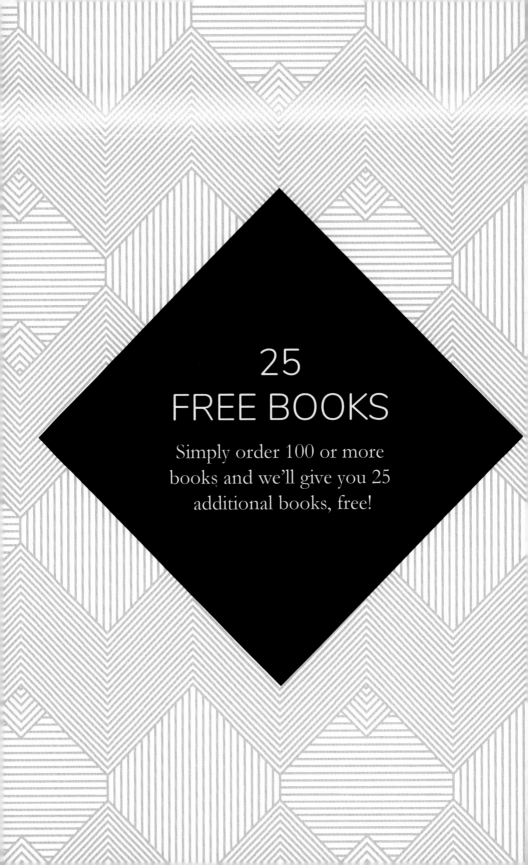

25
FREE BOOKS

Simply order 100 or more
books and we'll give you 25
additional books, free!

There have been many successful authors who have used Amazon's huge internet presence to make a nice profit selling their books. But for every success story, there are many, many stories of dashed hopes and lost profits. Amazon can be a great benefit to you as an author, but you need to do your homework before jumping in with both feet. Know your costs, track your sales, and keep on top of all the numbers, and you can make Amazon a useful partner.

Don't Let a Third Party Handle Your Amazon Sales.

Any seasoned author knows you should NEVER let a third party control your Amazon sales. If you're not comfortable filling out the forms and doing all the necessary steps to list your book on Amazon, you probably shouldn't be considering them as an outlet for your books.

Suppose your book has a list price of $30. Amazon Advantage charges a $29.95 annual fee (which seems very reasonable), plus 60% of the list price (which means you're helping Amazon make a lot of money, but you may not be making any for yourself).

Consider all of your costs. You still have to pay for the printing of the book, plus the cost of shipping it to Amazon. And this just gets your book onto Amazon's list of available books. They do not do any marketing for your book. You'll have to do that yourself.

Even in the best of situations, it can be difficult to make money selling your books through Amazon. Now that you see what your costs really are, you'll see that as the author and publisher, you MUST have full control over your Amazon contract. Otherwise, a third party will be taking an additional cut of the profits out of your already miniscule bottom line.

Amazon by the numbers

	Book Sold Thru Amazon at $30	Book Sold Thru Amazon at $28	Book Sold Yourself at $30
List Price	$ 30.00	$ 28.00	$ 30.00
Amazon's fee (60% of list)	-18.00	-16.80	-----
Printing cost per book	-10.00	-10.00	-10.00
Shipping cost/book to Amazon*	-2.00	-2.00	-0.75
Net profit per book	$ 1.50	$ 0.60	$ 19.25
Number of book sales needed to make $1,000 profit	667	1,667	52

* *Shipping costs vary because Amazon will only let you ship small quantities of books (sometimes just 5-10) until your sales volume warrants a higher inventory. The books that you sell yourself (at a book signing, for instance) can be shipped in larger quantities at a much lower cost per book.*

If someone offers to list the book on Amazon for you, you should be very suspicious. First of all, they are going to expect a percentage of each sale (which will come out of your 40%, not Amazon's 60%). Furthermore, the third party would have control over your book. There are so many reasons why THAT is a bad idea. Here are just a few:

A. This third party would receive the book payments from Amazon, and you'll have to go after THEM for YOUR payment. Getting your money from Amazon can be frustrating at times, but trying to get it from a third party might prove to be impossible. You won't have Amazon's sales records to back you up, either (the third party will have those).

B. This third party makes money with each copy of your book that is sold through Amazon. That sounds great to you, because they'll have incentive to increase your book sales. But one way they may increase those sales is to lower the list price on your book. Do you see what happens to your profits if they decide to drop the list price by just $2 down to $28 per book? (See the 2nd column from the chart on the previous page). Some authors do the math and realize that they're actually losing money with each book they sell through Amazon.

C. And on the off chance that your book gets picked up for a movie project, guess what? You can bet that third party is going to want a healthy cut of that, too.

Now all this does not mean that Amazon is a bad option for selling your book. You just need to be very careful. Set up the Amazon account yourself, keep careful track of what your ACTUAL costs will be for each book. Consider ordering in larger quantities to get a better price per book. We at 48 Hour Books can ship directly to Amazon, so you're not paying twice for shipping.

Determine what profit you want to be able to keep from each copy sold, and work the math backwards to arrive at a list price. This way, when you do get a sale through Amazon, you'll know that you're making a profit.

Use Amazon If You'd Like, but Concentrate Your Efforts Where Your Most Profitable Sales Are

Your greatest profit potential is by selling the books yourself, through your established networks and channels.

Augment these channels with your own website. If you don't know anything about websites, pay someone to set it up for you. There are lots of people who can create a website with complete ordering capabilities. But the important thing is, make sure YOU have full control. This doesn't mean you have to actually RUN the website; you can pay somebody to do that, too. But make sure you can FIRE them if you're not happy with what they're doing.

You can then market your book however you feel is appropriate, directing potential readers to your website to order. You should be able to achieve the same level of sales this way as through Amazon, and you'll keep virtually all the profits.

5

chapter five

How To Use Our Free Book Templates

4.25 x 7   5.5 x 8.5   6 x 9   8.5 x 11

We've created some free book templates that you can use when writing your book. They make it a little easier to set up and format it. Within each template, we've started with a few simple paragraph styles for you, and you're welcome to make whatever changes or adjustments you'd like. The templates are available on our website at www.48HrBooks.com/self-publishing/book-templates. They can be opened in Microsoft Word, Word Perfect, Pages, Open Office, or just about any word processing program. (If you're working in InDesign, you can place one of our templates into those programs. Be sure to carry over the paragraph styles that you used in Word directly into InDesign).

There are four different standard sizes of template: 4.25 x 7, 5.5 x 8.5, 6 x 9, and 8.5 x 11. If your book is going to be a different size, simply start with one of these standard templates, and adjust the page size as needed. It might be smart to change the page sizes before you begin typing, but you can change it later if you prefer. The book templates have virtually everything you'll need, from the Title Page to the Copyright Page, Dedication,

Table of Contents, Foreword, Preface, Introduction, and several chapters. Some of these you may not want to use, so you can just delete them. They all have placeholder text that you can replace with your own wording. For example, to replace the placeholder text for the book title, simply select that type and type your book title in place of it.

Microsoft Word is a nice program, but it does have some significant limitations. For example, you'll need to be careful when deleting type that might contain page breaks or carriage returns. If you have two consecutive paragraphs that are different styles, and you accidentally delete the carriage return in between them, the new larger paragraph is going to change to the style of the 2nd paragraph. That might be what you wanted, but if it's not, just choose the paragraph style that you want from the list under Paragraph Styles.

I suggest you learn the basics of Microsoft Word before trying to format your book. Pay special attention to working with Paragraph Styles. Using those can really make your life a lot easier. Remember to turn ON invisible characters (on the Home tab, under Paragraph group, choose "Show/Hide"), so you'll be able to see where you added a tab character or a carriage return, or if you've got extra spaces somewhere. Also, be sure to use Word's auto-save feature. You can set it to automatically save your file every 10-15 minutes, so you don't have to worry about losing a day's worth of work.

This is a paragraph symbol. Each symbol indicates where a new paragraph begins as a result of a carriage return. It will show up any time you hit the "return" or "enter" key on your keyboard while typing your book.

¶

There's lots of detailed help available from the "Help" section within the program itself. Another great source is to simply Google what you're having trouble with. For instance, google "adding page breaks in word" and you'll get several web pages that give you the answers you need, and it's all free! Are you looking for more in-depth video training? We highly recommend www.Lynda.com, a video training website. They have detailed training videos for Microsoft Word, Photoshop, InDesign, and many other programs. They charge a monthly fee, but (at least as of the writing of this book) you could sign up for a month, learn the basics of Word in a matter of hours, and— if you don't think you'll be using Lynda much after that—cancel at any time. They really do have some great training videos. We use it ourselves when training new people.

Use the "Styles" in Word to help design your book

37

"We used to have a sign at my work that read, 'cheap, fast, good. Pick two.' Meaning, if it was cheap and fast, it wouldn't be good, and if it were good and cheap, it wouldn't be fast. 48 Hour Books seems to have found a way to do all three; excellent customer service, fast, and a beautiful end product. I highly recommend them!"

- Larry M.

6

chapter six

Anatomy of A Book...

What are all the parts?

There are many different parts to a book, broken down into three main sections: Front Matter, Body, and Back Matter. And, of course, you have the front and back cover.

In this chapter, I'll try to explain each part, from front to back. Many of these are seldom used these days, but I'll mention them here anyway.

Front Cover:

We print all of our covers on full-color presses, so be as creative as you'd like with yours. You want your book to stand out from the crowd, but also look professional. Add some photography, but be careful not to make it too busy. You'll probably want your background artwork to bleed (extend all the way to the edges of the book), so be sure to add 1/8" extra on all four sides. For your title, choose a font that's easy to read, and try to make the cover design suggest the type of book that it is (mystery, memoir, spiritual, self-help, etc.).

While your finished cover will be one contiguous piece that combines back and spine and front, most authors find it easier to do each piece separately, which is fine with us. Unlike many of our competitors, we will gladly put the front and back covers together for you, and add the spine—all for free. This way, you can concentrate on designing the front cover first, then move on to the back cover. As for the spine, you can either create one yourself, or we'll add a spine for you (again, no charge). If you're creating your own spine, be sure to calculate the correct spine width. In most cases, you'll divide your page count by 440 to get the spine width. If you chose a special paper for the inside, that number will change.

Front Matter:

Much of the Front Matter of a book is not necessary. But, if you want to produce a book in the classic style of days gone by, you'll want to include most, if not all, of the following parts.

FLYSHEET: A blank sheet at the very front of the book. Another flysheet should go at the very end of the book as well.

HALF TITLE: This page contains the book title only. Nothing else—not the author's name, not even a subtitle.

FRONTICEPIECE: A decorative page that faces the Title page. Rarely used these days.

TITLE PAGE: Contains the Book Title, Subtitle and Author's name

COPYRIGHT PAGE: On the back of the Title Page is the Copyright Page. It should contain the copyright message, the publisher or author, a "stripped book" warning, and the ISBN number.

The U.S. Copyright Office handles copyrights in the United States. Here are a few of their answers to common questions:

WHAT IS COPYRIGHT?

Copyright is a form of protection grounded in the U.S. Constitution and granted by law for original works of authorship fixed in a tangible medium of expression. Copyright covers both published and unpublished works.

WHEN IS MY WORK PROTECTED?

Your work is under copyright protection the moment it is created and fixed in a tangible form that it is perceptible either directly or with the aid of a machine or device.

DO I HAVE TO REGISTER WITH YOUR OFFICE TO BE PROTECTED?

No. In general, registration is voluntary. Copyright exists from the moment the work is created. You will have to register, however, if you wish to bring a lawsuit for infringement of a U.S. work.

WHY SHOULD I REGISTER MY WORK IF COPYRIGHT PROTECTION IS AUTOMATIC?

There are a number of reasons to register your work. Many authors wish to have the facts of their copyright on the public record and have a certificate of registration. Registered works may be eligible for statutory damages and attorney's fees in successful litigation. Finally, if registration occurs within 5 years of publication, it is considered prima facie evidence in a court of law.

For further information about copyrighting, go to the U.S. Copyright office's official website, www.copyright.gov. **Here is a typical layout for a copyright page:**

DEDICATION PAGE: Here the book can be dedicated to the person or persons who helped or inspired the author.

TABLE OF CONTENTS: Usually lists chapters and their starting page. At the author's discretion, it can also include various other front and back matter, like the Preface, Introduction, Epilogue or Appendix.

LIST OF FIGURES, LIST OF TABLES: Usually used in technical writings, these lists allow the reader to find the figures and tables more efficiently.

FOREWORD: A foreword is written by somebody other than the author, and usually tells of some interaction between the writer of the foreword and the author during the writing of the book. Also, be sure to spell "foreword" properly. When it is a part of a book, as it is here, it's spelled "Foreword." When it's a direction of travel, it's spelled "Forward."

PREFACE: A preface follows the foreword, and is written by the author, and generally describes how the book was developed.

ACKNOWLEDGEMENTS: An expression of gratitude from the author for support in creating the book. This support usually comes in the form of either moral or financial support.

INTRODUCTION: Here the author states the goal or purpose of the book. More common with technical writings or essays than with novels.

PROLOGUE: A way of introducing the story, the prologue is usually in the voice of a character in the book, rather than the voice of the author.

Body of the book:

The main body of the book is broken down into chapters. It is up to the individual author to decide whether to have only a few long chapters, or to have many short chapters. While we usually want chapters to start on an odd (right-hand) page, how you treat your chapter breaks will often depend on how many chapters you have. The great writer Kurt Vonnegut would sometimes have nearly 100 chapters in a 300-page book. With new chapters starting every couple of pages, it didn't make sense to force them all to start on a right-hand page, so he simply let the chapters start wherever they fell on a page, and added a little space before each one.

The formatting of your chapters is up to you. You'll probably want your body copy to be fairly basic, with justified paragraphs, and first-line indents. You might treat your chapter breaks a little more creatively, though. In general, start each chapter near the middle of the page, with white space above. You might consider adding a small graphic in that space at the beginning of each chapter.

On our website, we have several examples of how some of today's bestselling authors chose to format their books. It's worth taking a look at how they chose to format their title page, chapter heads, and table of contents.

Back Matter:

Back matter has been largely overlooked in most modern novels. While an Epilogue is still fairly common, the other parts of the Back Matter are rarely used today.

EPILOGUE (OR EXTRO, OUTRO, OR CONCLUSION):
These are all terms for a final piece of a story, after the main action is concluded, that serves to bring some form of closure to the work.

AFTERWORD (OR POSTSCRIPT OR ADDENDUM):

Similar to the Foreword, the Afterword is often added to a re-issue of a book. It is usually written by someone other than the author, and may discuss the book in some historical context.

The following additional parts to the back matter are generally used for technical writing and non-fiction works.

APPENDIX: adds factual information

GLOSSARY: describes terms used in the book

BIBLIOGRAPHY: a list of books & other works used by the author

INDEX: cross-references important terms with their corresponding page numbers in the book

COLOPHON: describes production notes relevant to the book. It usually includes a list of type faces used, and can include technical details about how the book was laid out, printed and bound.

Back Cover:

Since the back cover is also printed full-color, you can use a color photo for an "About The Author" segment. Also, some authors will include a synopsis of the book, or use portions of a review that the book may have received.

The type on a spine should run from top to bottom. When designing your spine, you can create a separate file. Set the width to be as tall as your book. For example, if your book is 6 x 9, your inside pages are 6" wide, but your spine should be 9" wide. Then simply type your book title and author name left to right, center them and add a little space as needed. Your finished book will properly show the title and author running from top to bottom.

"Absolutely
5 stars across the
board. The process was
ridiculously easy from beginning to
end, and instead of having to wait weeks and
weeks for my shipment, I got them in 2 days?!?!
The Hi-Gloss was well worth it, my books are *stunning* and
all arrived in perfect unblemished condition. I sold out at my
book party and will have to order more. User friendly
site, INSTANT support from their team,
and thorough instructions. Can't
recommend 48 Hour Books
more!"

- Angelita G.

7

chapter seven

Writing and Editing Your Book

Formatting & Layout:
Write First, Format Later

Different authors have different writing styles, but they can all be broken down into two distinct groups:

Group A authors write in manuscript form, without any formatting. Since they are concentrating on the writing, and leaving the formatting for later, the words often flow more freely. When they've finished the manuscript, they'll go back and format it the way that they want it.

Group B authors write and format as they go. They set up their page size, margins, font choices, paragraph styles, etc. before they've typed a single chapter. They then match that format with each additional chapter throughout the writing process. By the time they've written the last chapter, their book is already in their desired form.

Which method works best? It's really just a matter of personal preference, but we do have a recommendation. We've found that concentrating on the writing first (Group A) usually helps speed up the creative process. You can focus on the story itself without the distraction of formatting getting in the way. Actually WRITING your book is the tough part. It's the part that you, and only you, are qualified to do, so concentrate your energies on the writing, and leave the formatting to the end. Below, we'll go over detailed instructions for formatting your manuscript. If it's too intimidating, or you just don't have the time, you can always let us do the formatting for you.

If you choose to write first and format later, here are a few tips to help you avoid some common mistakes:

1. A word processor is NOT a typewriter ... if you're "old school," and learned to type on a typewriter, you'll have to UNlearn a few of the old typing rules. (A) Never put two spaces after a sentence, (B) Never hit a carriage return at the end of each line, and (C) Never use multiple spaces for a first line indent.

2. A new paragraph should be indicated by either an indented first line (the preferred way), or an extra space between paragraphs (rarely used, and not recommended). However, you should never use both methods. Assuming you use the preferred method of indenting the first line, you've got a choice. You can either add a tab character at the front of every paragraph, or leave it off and take care of it universally when you do the formatting later. But either way, be sure to be consistent throughout.

3. Turn ON invisible characters (Ctrl-Shift-8). You'll see tiny dots for spaces, and a paragraph mark for each carriage return. If you're not used to seeing your work this way, it may take a little getting used to, but it really helps to find and eliminate potential problems. You can easily toggle this off and on by hitting Ctrl-Shift-8.

When you've finally finished your manuscript, you'll want to put it into a nice format. We at 48 Hour Books can do that for you, but you can also try it yourself. It's not very hard, and if you do it right, it'll save you some money. The following steps assume that you want a 6 x 9 book, and that you're using Microsoft Word. You can tweak these instructions for different sizes and for different programs.

1. MAKE A COPY OF YOUR WORD FILE, putting the original in a safe place. If you completely screw things up, you can always throw the backup away and go back to your original.

2. SET YOUR PAGE SIZE -- Maybe you typed it into a word processor (like Microsoft Word) using the standard 'Letter size' paper, but you want your book to be printed on half-size paper. Don't worry. There's an easy way to change it, without re-typing the entire book. Open the copy of your file and select "File > Page Setup." On the "Margins" tab, make sure it says "Apply to: Whole Document." Choose the "Paper" tab and change the paper size to 6" x 9." Go back to the "Margins" tab and change all 4 margins. While we recommend .75 on all 4 sides, you should certainly never go less than .5 for Top, Left and Right, and .75 for Bottom, to leave space for your page numbers. Hit "OK" and Word will reflow your text.

3. CHOOSE YOUR FONTS -- There are two basic styles of type: "serif" and "sans serif."

Serifs are those tiny tails on the letters, as pictured below

"Sans Serif" is from the French, meaning "without serif." Countless studies have shown that a serif font is much easier to read in paragraph form than a sans serif font. Therefore, not surprisingly, most books use a serif font for the body copy, like Times, in 10 or 11 pt., and a bold sans serif font for headlines and chapter titles. If your audience is older, you may want to use a slightly larger font to make it easier for them to read. It's your book, so the final decision lies with you. You can use whatever font you'd like, but there are certain accepted standards, and you should think twice before deviating from the norm.

4. CREATE YOUR PARAGRAPH STYLES -- Some people are intimidated by this step, but they shouldn't be. It's actually very simple. It should take about 5 minutes to learn, and it will save you dozens of hours down the road. Learn to use Paragraph Styles, and always make any format changes on those Styles—not in the individual paragraphs themselves. This will also make it easy for you to make wholesale changes to your format in a matter of seconds.

    In most books, the overwhelming majority of paragraphs use a single style. In addition, there might be two or three (or maybe several) other paragraph styles for chapter heads, subheads, pull quotes, etc. Make a short list of YOUR different paragraph styles. Your first should be a "my body copy" paragraph style. Take a couple of minutes to format this style exactly the way you want it. It's far more efficient, and much more accurate, to format the paragraph STYLE one time, than to have to format each individual paragraph separately. When setting up your Paragraph Style, choose your preferred font, size, justification, line spacing, spacing between paragraphs, widow and orphan control, hyphenation, etc. It's your book, so if you want to be different, go right ahead. Here are our suggestions for each of the main choices you'll have to make:

    •   FONT: Times New Roman, Regular (not Bold or Italic). There are, of course, many other serif fonts. Just be careful not to pick one that's so ornate that it's difficult to read.

    •   SIZE: Generally between 10 pt. and 12 pt., but it's really up to you. You may want much larger type for a children's book.

- JUSTIFICATION: Normally "Justified," which means that the type is even on both the left and the right edges. Poetry books should be flush left.

- INDENT: For your body copy, you'll want zero for both left and right indents, but you may want a first-line indent of .188 or .25. If you want one of your other paragraph styles to be indented 1/2" more than your body copy, here's where you'll set that indent.

- LINE SPACING: Select "Multiple" at 1.2 or 1.25.

- SPACING BETWEEN PARAGRAPHS: For body copy, make this zero. For your headers and sub-heads, you may want to make it approximately the height of one line.

- WIDOW AND ORPHAN CONTROL: Turn it ON. See below for an explanation.

- HYPHENATION: Turn it ON. See below for an explanation.

- PAGE BREAK BEFORE: Definitely turn this OFF for your body copy, but you'll probably want it ON for your Chapter heads. Having it on will automatically move each chapter head to the next page.

Create all of your other paragraph styles in a similar fashion. To speed things along, you can make a copy of the "my body copy" style that you just created above, and name it "my chapter head." Next, modify that copy by changing the font, size, line justification and line spacing as needed. Do the same for any other special paragraph styles that you may want in your book.

5. SELECT ALL in your manuscript and change the entire file to "my body copy." That should take care of the majority of your book.

6. NOW YOU'LL JUST NEED TO... go through your book one more time, changing the few special paragraphs into their desired paragraph styles. Be sure to fix any awkward breaks that may have been created by these changes.

Look through your book and see if there are any minor formatting changes that you'd like to make. If there are, be sure to ONLY make the changes to the PARAGRAPH STYLES, not to the individual paragraphs. For example, if you decide to change your font, you can make that change once in the Paragraph Style for "my body copy," and it will change your entire book automatically.

Turn ON "Widow and Orphan Control"

Widows and Orphans are the lines at the beginning or end of a paragraph, which are left dangling at the top or bottom of a page, separated from the rest of the paragraph. Publishers work hard to eliminate all widows and orphans. Microsoft Word (and just about any good word processing program) has a Widow and Orphan control feature. Be sure to turn that ON for your body copy. As your text flows from page to page, if there is a paragraph that splits awkwardly, Word will correct it, making sure there are no widows or orphans. For example, let's say you have a paragraph that is 6 lines long, and there is only room for 5 lines at the bottom of the page. Rather than splitting it after 5 lines, leaving a widow at the top of the next page, Word will split it after 4 lines, so two lines get moved to the top of the next page. Similarly, if you have a 4 line paragraph and only one line fits at the bottom of the page, Word will push the entire paragraph to the next page. By necessity, this will sometimes cause the bottoms of text blocks to vary slightly from page to page. This is normal, and is the correct way to format, rather than suffering with widows and orphans.

For your special paragraph styles, if these paragraphs aren't crossing from one page to the next, it shouldn't matter whether it's ON or OFF.

Turn ON Hyphenation

You should also make sure that hyphenation is turned ON in the "my body text" paragraph style. This will eliminate many of the word spacing issues where words on a line are separated by spaces that seem too big. This is caused by the following word being too long to fit on that line. It is forced down to the next line, and the other words are spread out to fill the line, causing those large gaps. If you allow Word to hyphenate, it can probably fit half of that word on the above line, thereby reducing the large gaps. It's got a built-in dictionary, so it knows where to properly hyphenate just about any word, and you can even tell it not to hyphenate words that are capitalized.

Add Page Breaks between Chapters

You rarely want to add page breaks inside a chapter, but you will want to add a page break at the end of each chapter. You can either do that manually as you type, or you can do it universally by adding a Page Break to the front of your "chapter head" paragraph style. When modifying your "chapter head" paragraph style, you'll find a checkbox for adding a page break before the paragraph. Turn that ON, and all of your chapter heads will start on the following page.

The difference between "Editing" and "Formatting"

The simple answer is that editing is part of writing your book, and formatting is part of printing your book. So you are responsible for the editing, and we can help you with the formatting if you wish.

Editing concerns the content, and it doesn't really matter how it looks on the page. An editor will read through your entire manuscript, correcting spelling, syntax, and grammar mistakes, checking for continuity throughout your story, and working to improve the clarity and readability of your book. This should always be done in collaboration with the author. For several weeks during the editing process, you and the editor will work in tandem to clean up your manuscript as best you can. You can either hire a copy editor, ask a friend or relative to help, or do it yourself.

If you choose to be your own editor, you'll need to read your manuscript through the eyes of your prospective reader. Slow down and read it analytically. You wrote this, so you know what it's supposed to say. By reading it slowly, you might catch minor grammatical errors that you didn't see originally.

Formatting is the process of making the words that you've typed look good. It has nothing to do with content—it's strictly about looks. The objective is to get a book that looks great and is consistent throughout. Chapter headings should all look the same and paragraph styles should all be uniform from the beginning of your book to end.

At 48 Hour Books, we can format your book if you'd like. Just send us a Word document (or other word processor file), and we'll format it to look great. We're not editing—we don't read your entire book or analyze the content. If we're going to print your books in 48 hours, as well as dozens of other authors' books every day, we simply don't have the time to read your entire book and suggest editorial changes.

CHOOSE A DESIGNER STYLE

JOHN GRISHAM (THE FIRM) PAGE EXAMPLES

Title Page   "Chapter" Headings   Lefthand Page

8

chapter eight

Creating a PDF File of Your Book

This is only if you've formatted your inside pages exactly the way that you want them. If you want us to do the reformatting for you, send us your Word document or other word processing file.

1. Make sure your page size and margins are correct.
2. Most word processing programs will let you select "File > Save as PDF" or "File > Print > Save as PDF," or "File > Export to PDF."

If yours doesn't, try downloading and installing "doPDF," then select it as your printer. When you 'print' to doPDF, it will actually create a PDF file for you. It gives you an option of where to save it on your computer, so pay attention to where the PDF file gets saved.

3. **Two settings to check:**

   - Embed all of your fonts
   - Do not downsample your graphics

Double-check your files
before sending them to us

You've probably spent many months, even years, writing your book. We HIGHLY recommend that you spend an extra hour or two looking it over one last time before you send it to us. To avoid possible charges for corrections down the road, you really want to get it right the first time.

Does it have to be perfect? Well, no. You want it as close as reasonably possible, but there have been plenty of best-sellers with typos, imperfect grammar, mis-registration, poor photo reproduction, etc. There have even been instances where the main character's name changes abruptly in the middle of the book ... no explanation, clearly an editing mistake, but it didn't keep the books from selling many thousands of copies.

If you're waiting until it's absolutely perfect, you may never get it printed. Our best recommendation would be to create an MVP (Minimum Viable Product), then work to improve it along the way. You may know that it needs a little more work, but it's probably 95% of the way there, so it's still a great book, and your readers should certainly get their money's worth.

Your goal may be to write a best-seller, but there's nothing wrong with doing a first printing, even if there are a couple of minor flaws. This way, you'll get it out to the public early, it'll buy you some extra time to fix those imperfections, and you just might get some interest from one of the big publishers in the meantime.

IMPORTANT: Keep in mind, we print directly from the files you send us, so if there's a mistake in your file, that same mistake will be in every one of your books. So check your files, then check them again, then have somebody else check them ... you get the idea.

9

chapter nine

Placing an Order

SAMPLE: 80# Smooth Cover
(uncoated)

While there are dozens of decisions to make when placing your order, we make it as simple as possible. We break down all the choices for you, describe them, and offer suggestions. Each decision has a "Help" button that goes into greater detail about your choices. And, of course, if you're still not sure which is best for you, we're available to answer any questions you have. We'll even walk you through the ordering process over the phone if needed, a benefit that many first-timers find invaluable.

The following is a quick breakdown of the choices you'll make.

Just The Basics: Binding Type

We offer four (4) different binding styles: perfect bound (paper-back book), hard cover (case bound book), spiral coil bound, and saddle-stitched (folded sheets with 2 staples on the fold). The overwhelming majority of books at bookstores are perfect bound. So, not surprisingly, most of the books we print are perfect bound. They're the

fastest option, the least expensive option, and what's most in demand from your readers. Hard cover books suggest a slightly higher quality of book. They're more durable than paperbacks, but are a little more expensive and take a few days longer to produce.

Some authors want both perfect bound and hard cover. We can do that, too. Simply choose perfect bound here, then later in the ordering process you'll be asked if you'd like to convert some to hard cover. If you decide to do this, keep in mind that we do require a minimum of 10 books of each binding type selected. Spiral coil bound books are excellent for cookbooks, workbooks, calendars, directories, or any other type of book that you want to lay completely flat on the counter. Finally, saddle-stitched books are generally for very thin booklets (36 pages or less). Financial reports, instruction manuals, and catalogs might be saddle-stitched.

Book Size

Our most popular book size is 5.5 x 8.5, so it's selected by default, but we offer 13 more standard sizes, and can do virtually any special size you want, up to 11 x 11 square. Most books are portrait size, with the height being more than the width, and the binding on the LONG edge. We have 4 standard portrait sizes.

Landscape sizes are wider than they are tall, with the binding on the SHORT edge. We have 5 standard landscape sizes. And square

books are just that: square! Their height and width are the same. We have 5 standard square sizes.

What if you want a Special Size? No problem! Simply choose the next size larger (one big enough that YOUR size could fit inside it), then tell us the width and height of your book, and on which edge the binding will be.

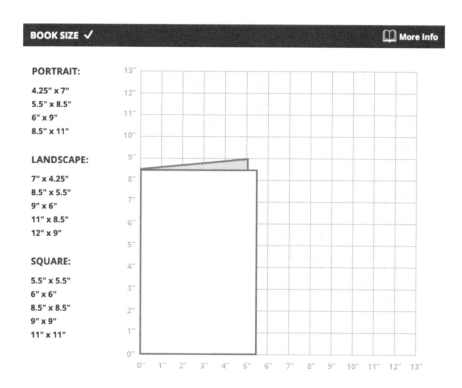

Number of Pages

Tell us the number of pages in your book, how many black-and-white and how many color. Keep in mind that we're counting PAGES, and not sheets of paper. Let's say, for example, you printed out your book on your desktop printer. You printed it 2-sided, and it took 70 sheets of paper. That makes it's a 140-page book, so your total number of pages should equal 140.

When entering COLOR PAGES, do NOT include your cover. We always print your cover in full color for free. So here, you're only counting INSIDE pages that you want printed in color.

Color pages are more expensive to produce, so if you're trying to keep your costs down, consider reducing the number of color pages. You may have several pages with colored highlights that don't really need to be in full color. We can convert those highlights to a shade of gray, so they'll qualify as black-and-white pages, saving you money. You may also be able to reduce the number of color pages by grouping your color photos together on less pages.

Quantity

This one's pretty simple ... just enter the number of books you want to order.

Of course, we also recommend ordering a few extra books, because you'll often get additional requests for them. It's more cost-effective to order a few extras on your initial order than to place a second order for 10 books later.

Once we have these four elements (Binding Type, Book Size, Number of Pages, and Quantity of Books), we can give you a price. You've still got plenty of other options that you may want to add, from special features like foil stamping or adding a special cover, to Rush services or expedited shipping.

Inside Paper Choices

We have several different papers available for the inside pages of your book. We've divided them into Offset Paper and Coated Paper.

Paper Type	Weight	ppi (Pages per inch)
Bright White Offset	60#	440
	70#	378
	80#	330
Cream Offset	60#	440
	70#	378
Silk Text (white)	80#	440
	100#	352
Gloss Text (white)	80#	480
	100#	384

Under Offset Paper, you have the choice of either Bright White or Cream.

BRIGHT WHITE OFFSET is our standard book paper. It is a smooth, uncoated sheet, available in 60#, 70#, or 80#.

CREAM OFFSET is also a smooth, uncoated sheet, but in a cream color, which adds a little richness to your book. It's available in 60#, or 70#.

Under Coated Paper, you have the choice of either Silk Text or Gloss Text.

SILK TEXT has a soft, beautiful silk finish. Sometimes called "Matte" or "Satin." It's also been described as a 'low gloss'. Full-color photos look great on Silk Text, without the glare that you'll get with Gloss Text. It's available in 80# or 100#.

We also offer GLOSS TEXT, in 80# or 100#. For decades, gloss text was the standard for full-color printing. And while it still looks great, many authors today are switching to "Silk" text.

The PPI number that is listed on each paper choice in the chart on page 69 stands for "Pages Per Inch." Our standard 60# Offset is 440 PPI, so a 440-page book would be about an inch thick. A 220 page book would be about 1/2 inch thick. The lower the PPI, the thicker the paper is.

Cover Material Choices

Based on your choice of binding, we have different cover materials available. Here's a quick explanation of each option:

Cover Options for Perfect Bound, Spiral Coil Bound, or Saddle-Stitched Books:

STANDARD 10 PT. C1S - A heavy 10 mil cover paper, with a smooth, hard surface for the outside and uncoated surface on the inside. You'll have a choice of three different coatings: Gloss UV is our default (*See chapter 1 for a sample*), but you can also choose Silk Laminate (our personal favorite - *see chapter 3 for a sample*), or Hi-Gloss Laminate (*see chapter 5 for a sample*).

12 PT. C1S - Just like the 10 pt. above, but 20% heavier. It's a 12 mil cover paper, with a smooth, hard surface for the outside and uncoated surface on the inside. And, just like the 10 pt. above, you'll be able to choose your coating: Gloss UV, Silk Laminate, or Hi-Gloss Laminate. (*See chapter 7 for a sample*).

80# SMOOTH COVER - A heavy (11 mil) cover paper, with a smooth finish. No coating, no glossing ... for authors looking for a more basic, earthier feel for their covers. (*See chapter 9 for a sample*).

80# LINEN COVER - Similar to the 80# Uncoated Cover above, this has a subtle linen finish. It's about 9.5 mil thick, which is still plenty thick enough. No coating, but the linen finish adds to the richness of your cover. (*See chapter 11 for a sample*).

LEATHERETTE COVER - An acrylic-coated paper with a pronounced leather embossed finish. Leatherette can't be printed on. It's either blank or Diamond 3D Foil stamped. (*See beginning of chapter 13 for a sample*). Available in the following colors:

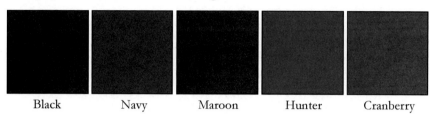

| Black | Navy | Maroon | Hunter | Cranberry |

Cover Options for Hard Cover Books:

All of our hard cover materials are eventually wrapped around heavy, warp-resistant book boards, to make a very durable, hard cover book.

STANDARD COVER - We print your full-color cover on 100# Gloss Text, then laminate it with your choice of Silk Laminate or Hi-Gloss Laminate.

LEATHERETTE - An acrylic-coated paper with a pronounced leather embossed finish. Leatherette can't be printed on. They're either blank (usually with a printed dust jacket), or Diamond 3D Foil stamped. (*See beginning of chapter 13 for a sample*. Color options shown above).

LEATHER - Our 'top-of-the-line' cover option, this is a bonded leather made of 100% cowhide leather fibers. Its leather embossed finish makes a beautiful, rich-looking book cover. It may be a little more expensive than our other luxury covers, but it's worth it. It can be foil stamped or left blank (usually with a printed dust jacket). Available in the following colors:

| Black | Navy | Burgundy | Forest | Brown |

PEARL LINEN (CLOTH) - A beautiful yet economical cover material with a pronounced linen weave. Can be foil stamped or left blank (usually with a printed dust jacket). These high-quality covers are available in several bright, vibrant colors:

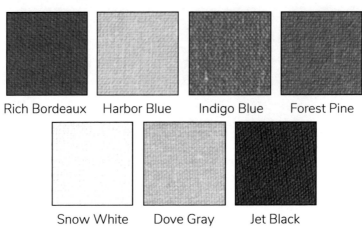

Rich Bordeaux   Harbor Blue   Indigo Blue   Forest Pine

Snow White   Dove Gray   Jet Black

Diamond 3D Covers:
Foil, Clear, & Smart Textures

This is not just a 3D effect. It's actual 3D printing that you can see ... and FEEL!

Available on any binding type with a Gloss UV, Silk Laminate, or Leatherette cover stock, Diamond 3D is a clear coating that is raised up from the surface of your cover. Our graphic designers will choose a couple of elements on your cover (usually your book title, plus a few smaller areas - depending on your artwork) to highlight with this exclusive technique. *Check out the cover of this book to see an example of our Diamond 3D Clear and Diamond 3D Foil -- shown with Silk Laminate.*

DIAMOND 3D FOIL - Nothing says 'Best Seller' like foil stamping. This is a raised metallic foil coating that can be used to highlight elements of your book cover to really catch the eye. Currently available in gold, silver, red, or blue.

DIAMOND 3D CLEAR - a clear, raised coating that is printed on top of your artwork to give it a high-gloss raised "3D" effect that you can see and feel! Since it's clear, it accentuates all of the printed colors underneath it, turning any cover into one that will really grab your reader's attention.

DIAMOND 3D SMART TEXTURES - these use the same technology as our Diamond 3D Clear coating. We'll apply one of our available textures to your entire cover to imitate the feel of a non-paper cover (such as linen or leather). Our graphic designers will customize the background to make sure printed elements of your cover aren't overshadowed and that all of your text is still legible.

Popular options:
Traditional Foil Stamping

If you've selected either our Leather or Cloth cover, don't worry - we also offer traditional foil stamping so you can include text or a design on your book cover.

In this case, we custom order a die using your artwork. We take metallic foil and fuse it onto the sheet with high heat and high pressure. It adds shimmer and richness to your cover, setting you apart from the crowd.

For traditional foil stamping, you'll be asked to select a die size. Measuring your die size is actually very simple, but if you're still not quite sure, just guess at a size, and we'll check it for you.

Make a mock-up of your cover. Draw an imaginary rectangle around the area to be foil stamped. If you want it on the spine or back cover, be sure your mock-up includes these areas, too. Measuring in inches, multiply width x height of your rectangle to get the square inches.

- If it's 5" wide and 3" tall, your die size will be 5 x 3 = 15 square inches.
- If it's 2" wide and 8" tall, your die will be 2 x 8 = 16 square inches.
- If it's 8" wide and 10" tall, your die will be 8 x 10 = 80 square inches.

We've made it simple by having four die sizes:
- Small (less than 27 square inches)
- Medium (between 27 and 54 square inches)
- Large (between 54 and 81 square inches)
- Extra Large (over 81 square inches)

If you're ordering a reprint and we've already got your die from the previous order, still select the die size here, but tell us "use the existing die" in the "Comments" section later on in the order process.

And finally, if you've selected foil stamping, you'll be asked to select a foil color.

Dust Jackets

If you selected hard cover books, you can choose to order dust jackets for your books. Most hard cover books have full-color dust jackets to protect the cover, and serve as a bookmark for your readers. We print dust jackets in full-color on 100# Gloss Text, then laminate them with your choice of Silk Laminate or Hi-Gloss Laminate.

Since we can't print on leather, cloth, or leatherette covers, you may decide to include photos or more intricate designs on a dust jacket instead. On the flaps, you can add an 'About the Author' section, a few quick quotes from book reviewers, or maybe a teaser or synopsis of your book.

So What's Our "Top-of-the-Line" Cover?

For hard cover books: foil stamp our leather book cover with the title and author's name, then add a full-color dust jacket with Diamond 3D Foil.

For all other books: choose Diamond 3D Foil on either a full-color cover (with Silk or Hi-Gloss Laminate), or on our leatherette cover.

Printed Proof -
Think of it Like "Book Insurance"

This is our most commonly-ordered option—and with good reason. On all new orders, you'll always receive a PDF Proof to approve. After you've approved that, we can send you a Printed Proof: one complete book, printed and bound like your full order will be. It's really the only fool-proof way to check color, since colors often look different on your back-lit computer screen than they do when you print them on paper. Many people find it easier to catch spelling or other errors when viewing an actual book. If there's a mistake in your files, wouldn't it be better to catch it on your Printed Proof rather than after your entire order is printed?

We highly recommend a Printed Proof, especially for first-time authors. It can save you a lot of money. Getting a Printed Proof can save you hundreds, even thousands, of dollars.

ISBNs and Barcodes

An ISBN is a 10- or 13-digit "International Standard Book Number." (ISBNs issued before 2007 are 10 digits, and ISBNs issued after January 1, 2007 are 13 digits. Both are valid formats). Bookstores and book distributors use this number to be sure they're ordering the correct book. If you're planning on selling your books in stores, you'll need an ISBN. If your book doesn't have an ISBN, bookstores (including online bookstores) may not carry it.

Each version of your book (paperback, hard cover, ePub, MOBI, PDF, audiobook, etc.) has its own unique ISBN, which will appear on all copies of that version. If you order 1,000 books, you'll still only need the one ISBN. Even reprints will use the same ISBN. Only if you make substantial revisions to a title will it require a new number. So, if you're only printing one version, you'll only need one ISBN. If you're printing both a perfect bound version and a hard cover version, and offering two different eBook versions (ePub and MOBI), you'll need 4 ISBNs just for that one title. If that's the case, it will be smartest to order your ISBNs in blocks of 10, 100, or even 1,000. The cost per ISBN drops significantly if you order them in larger blocks. Keep in mind that once you've assigned these numbers to a particular binding type and title, they cannot be re-used.

Our ISBN packages include a free barcode for each ISBN. We'll provide you with detailed instructions for updating your book listings at BooksInPrint.com, where all bookstores and book distributors go to find your book. We receive ISBNs the day after they are ordered, so in some cases, it may add a day to your order.

Barcode only

If you already have the ISBN, and just need a barcode to go along with it, we can handle that. Just click the 'Yes' box here and provide us with the ISBN. We also embed the price of the book in the barcode, so either (a) give us your selling price, or (b) tell us 'no price'. Hint: if you haven't decided on a price yet, or think you might be changing the price in the future, tell us 'no price'. That way, you're not locked in to a particular price.

Design Work for Inside Pages (Reformatting)

If you can send us a Print-Ready PDF that has your correct page size and the fonts are embedded, select 'No Thanks', and there's no charge. But if you want us to reformat your inside pages for you, select "Yes" and we'll show you several sample designs that best selling authors have used. If it works for them, it should work for you. Look over the sample pages, find one that you like, then select that author and book. We'll use their book design as a guide when reformatting your book. IMPORTANT: If you want us to reformat your book for you, you need to send us a Word document or other word processor file. We cannot reformat a PDF file.

Cover Design

If you've already got your cover designed, you're all set. There's no charge, just select 'None' here.

If you want some help with a cover design, you've got two other options:

OUR 'ECONOMY' CREATE-A-COVER gives you a professional-looking book cover for a fraction of the cost. We have several templates for you to look at. Simply choose a template that you like, choose a color combination, and then send us any elements (photos, graphics, and type). We'll put them all together according to your instructions, and send you a PDF Proof. We even include one set of changes or corrections for free.

OUR 'CUSTOM' COVER DESIGN is a little more elaborate. One of our graphic designers will give you a call to discuss your book cover. We'll get your input, then create a couple of rough drafts of covers. Simply let us know what you like or dislike about each of the rough drafts. We'll make whatever changes you need and come up with a cover design you'll be happy with.

Convert 25 to Hard Cover

If you've selected perfect binding, spiral coil binding, or saddle-stitching, you'll be given the option to convert 25 books to hard cover. We do require that you order at least 10 of each binding type, so this option will only appear if you're ordering 35 or more books.

We can "convert" 10 or more books to hard cover on any non-hard cover order. These are not additional books. For example, if you order 50 perfect bound books and opt to convert 25 of those to hard cover, you'll receive 25 perfect bound books and 25 hard cover books to total 50 books. Compared to our regular perfect bound prices, hard cover books are typically $10 more per book, but we do offer a special when converting 25 to hard cover: $210, which will save $40.

Keep in mind that hard cover books take 5 days in production, so we'll ship you perfect bound books as soon as they are ready, and send the hard cover books in a second shipment, a few days later.

Inside Cover Printing

This is pretty self-explanatory. Our standard book covers are blank on the inside, but if you'd like some printing on either the inside front cover or inside back cover, just check one of the "Yes" boxes here, for either black-and-white or full-color.

Please note: hard cover books cannot have printing on the inside cover. Our hard cover books include white or cream end sheets that are glued to the inside of the front and back covers.

eBooks

We offer fast and affordable eBook Conversion, including an 'Economy' option that is perfect for most books.

We create two different sets of files:

(a) MOBI format (for Amazon), which should ONLY be installed and read on a Kindle, and

(b) ePub format (non-Amazon, for the rest of the world), which should ONLY be installed and read on any one of dozens of other eReaders (iPad, Nook, etc.). You should NOT attempt to read these files on a computer, even with eBook simulators.

We don't use a computer program that spits out generic eBook files that will have mistakes throughout. Your files are always converted manually, so a human is actually looking at your files and hand-making all the adjustments required. The added care and crafts-manship shows in the finished product. And of course, we include a jpg image of the front cover on every order. You'll want that for dis-playing your eBook online.

Simply plug in how many you have of each of the following:

- pages
- footnotes or endnotes
- pictures, graphics and charts

We'll calculate the cost for you, and you can decide whether or not you want us to create the eBooks for you.

Diecut Tabs

If you're ordering spiral coil bound books, you can add diecut tabs to your book as section dividers. You've got a choice of black-and-white or full-color, and the tabs can be either one-sided or two-sided. Let us know how many tabs you'd like, and how many in a 'bank', and we'll include the tabs in your proof.

One-sided Printing

We RARELY print books one-sided. You would have to have a very good reason to print your book this way. However, if you do want your book printed one-sided, check the 'Yes' box. One-sided printing is a little more expensive ... because even though you've got the same amount of printing, you're using twice as much paper. It also doubles the weight, so shipping is more expensive, too.

Perforated Pages

We RARELY perforate pages in a book, so you probably don't need this. But if you do want perforated pages, we can do it. Tell us how many pages are to be perforated, and what page numbers.

Because there are 2 pages per sheet, you should always enter an EVEN number of pages. For example, if you had 3 SHEETS that need to be perforated. You might enter: '6', in the first box, and 'pages 13-14, 27-28, 109-110' in the second box.

Scanning

If you need any hi-resolution scanning done, we've got 3 different options. Each option is described below. Simply choose the one that's right for you.

Scan Wording as an Image - Lowest cost. We scan all of the pages of a book. Keep in mind, this just produces a 'picture' of each page, so they can't be edited at all.

OCR Scan - We start by scanning pages of a book. Then, using Optical Character Recognition, we convert the 'picture' of each page into a fully-editable Word document. With the Word document, we'll be able to make any corrections or changes that you want to make. A word of warning: Optical Character Recognition is incredibly accurate, but IT IS NOT PERFECT. You'll want to read through the entire file looking for errors. But that's a lot easier than re-typing the entire book, right?

Scan Photos - We'll scan your photos in hi-resolution. Just let us know how many photos you want scanned in black and white, and how many photos you want scanned in full-color. You'll also want to send us instructions for photo placement.

Computer Time

If you know that your order is going to require some special attention, you can indicate how much you're willing to spend on it. If the work we need to do is liable to go over that allotted amount, we'll contact you and get your permission to continue.

Finishing up

The last steps are pretty straightforward. Simply enter information about yourself, shipping instructions, and payment information. We take checks, Paypal, wire transfer, and the four major credit cards (American Express, Visa, Master Card, and Discover).

As soon as your order is submitted, you'll be able to upload files directly to our website. Our File Upload page allows you to either drag-and-drop files or browse your computer to find the files that you want to send. When you've added them all, hit "Start Upload." Depending on the size of your files, it may take some time to upload, so be patient. If you've got extremely large files, we can send you a link to our file-sharing site as an alternative. If you've got a slow connection, you can put your files on a thumb drive and ship them to us (Next Day Air if you're in a hurry, regular mail or UPS Ground if you're not in a hurry).

"48
Hour Books
is impressive end to
end. Small businesses with
personal service are closing, leaving us
at the mercy of very large impersonal Internet
corporations. That's absolutely NOT the case here! 48
Hour Books uses a sophisticated blend of people and technology
that places real people precisely where they are needed and
lets machines do the rest. The founders have four
decades experience in the printing business
and have done a creative job of
merging the new and
old processes. Their
team is a pleasure to work
with. I was guided through the
process--no pressured upsell, just polite
suggestions to avoid mistakes and improve the product
at minimal extra cost. If you say no, they respectfully accept
that. Quick responses to messages on their site or phone calls--
all this at a very reasonable price and delivered on time
as promised, thanks to the technology! Get
as much or as little help as you need.
If you're a first time author,
they're perfect! "

- John W.

10

chapter ten

How It Works

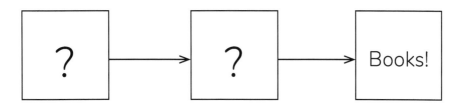

A Simplified Flowchart

Many first-time authors want to know what our process is. The following two pages contain a flowchart that shows what happens after you place your order and send us your files, along with a quick explanation of each step of that flowchart.

Remember that you'll either send us PDF files for the inside of your book (if they're formatted correctly), or Word documents if you want us to format for you. Cover files do not have to be PDFs: we also accept: .tif, .jpg, or .png.

We've tried to make every step quick and easy, from placing your order, to uploading files, to viewing your PDF proof and signing off. If you run into trouble at any step of the way, we encourage you to call or email us with any questions. We can help you get past any trouble you have. Computers are wonderful things, but they don't always do what we expect them to do. If you have trouble with your order or with your files, let us know. We can help.

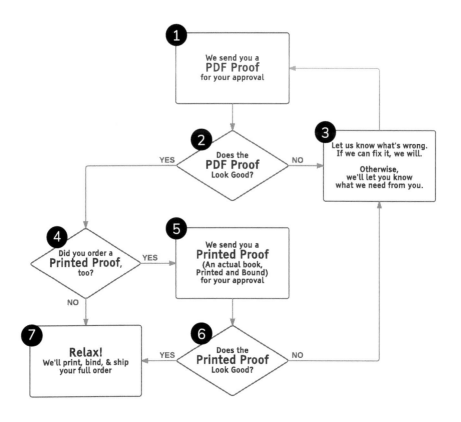

1. WE SEND YOU A PDF PROOF TO APPROVE.

2. LOOK IT OVER CAREFULLY. If there are any mistakes, those same mistakes will be on all of your books, so don't approve it unless it's right. For example, if you ordered an ISBN and barcode, but there's just a white box but no barcode on your cover, don't approve it ... let us know that it's missing!

3. IF YOU REJECT YOUR PDF PROOF, just let us know what's wrong with it, and we'll fix it if we can, or we'll let you know what we need from you. Then we'll send you another PDF Proof, so go back to **STEP 2**. When you're happy with the PDF Proof, simply log onto your account and approve it.

4. IF YOU DID NOT ORDER A PRINTED PROOF, go to **STEP 7**.

IF YOU DID ORDER A PRINTED PROOF, go to **STEP 5**.

5. WE'LL PRINT, BIND & SHIP YOUR PRINTED PROOF to you. This is a single copy of your book as an extra review and approval step .

    A Printed Proof is great for several reasons:
    - you'll see the precise colors on your cover and inside pages
    - it's easier to find errors on a printed book than on a PDF
    - think of it like "Book Insurance" ... it's much better to find errors on a single book than on your full order.

6. AGAIN, BE SURE TO LOOK IT OVER CAREFULLY. You've already approved the PDF Proof so, hopefully, there won't be any other errors. But if there are, simply reject the Printed Proof, and let us know what's wrong with it. We'll send you another PDF Proof, so go back to **STEP 2**. (Most people don't need a 2nd Printed Proof, but we do give you that option if you want it). When you've approved your final proof, go to **STEP 7**.

7. RELAX! We're printing and binding your full order. The order will update on your account to show the ship date. Or just call or email us, and we'll find it for you.

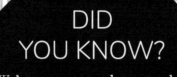

DID
YOU KNOW?

We're very proud to say that
we print and bind all of our books in
the USA. In fact, up until November 2019,
everything was done in-house in Akron, OH.
In 2019, we opened a second location in Las Vegas, NV.
This saves our West Coast clients up to 3 days in
shipping time! Both locations are exclusively
owned and operated by 48 Hour
Books—so you can trust that
your books are always in
good hands.

11

chapter eleven

So You've Approved Your Proofs. Now What?

SAMPLE: 80# Linen Cover
(uncoated)

The Clock Starts

After you have approved your proofs, we will let you know if there is a balance due on the order. Remember, we don't start printing your order until it's paid in full. We'll never charge your card without your permission, so be sure to check your email often (or log in to your account to check the status on a regular basis). Once it's paid in full, the "48 Hour Books" clock starts ticking. That means that you can relax, because your work is done.

Now it's up to us. Here's a very quick description of the various steps involved in producing your books. Each of these steps is actually a whole lot more complicated than described here, but this will give you a basic idea of what's going on.

The first thing we have to do is to print your books. We print the inside pages separately from the cover. The covers are printed on one of our full-color digital presses. If you chose a coating (Gloss UV, Silk Laminate, or

Hi-Gloss Laminate), we apply that to the covers after they're printed. Then, the covers are trimmed down in preparation for binding.

For the inside pages, if you've got color pages, they'll be printed on one of our full-color digital presses. Black-and-white pages will be printed on one of our black-and-white digital presses. Regardless of which press we choose, the books come out of the press as a complete 'book block,' which is one complete set of the inside pages of your book, fully collated, but with no cover.

We then take these book blocks and trim them to slightly larger than the finished size. For example, if you ordered a 6 x 9 book, we'll trim your book block to roughly 6 1/4 x 9 1/4. It's not trimmed to the actual finished size until the very end.

The next step varies slightly, depending on the type of binding.

A. For perfect bound books, the next step is to affix the covers to the book blocks. This is done on one of our high-speed perfect binders. Each book block is clamped tightly, the spine is milled to provide a rougher surface for the glue to penetrate. Glue is applied to the spine itself, and to each side of the spine. This provides for a much more durable bind. Meanwhile, the covers are fed into the binder and are scored with a double-hinge score, one set of scores at the spine, and another set (the hinge) about 1/4" away from the spine on front and back cover. Next, the covers are stuck to the book block, and are clamped in place to allow the glue to begin to cure.

After the glue has cured enough to trim them, the books are fed into a 3-knife trimmer, which trims the top, bottom, and face in one operation, leaving you with a beautifully-finished perfect bound book.

B. For coil bound books, the book blocks are sent through a high-speed precision punch, which punches the holes along the spine. Then, the plastic coil is added by machine, and the ends are cut and crimped, so they won't unravel.

C. For hard cover books, the book blocks are bound to endsheets, and then 3-knife trimmed. After your covers have been glued and wrapped around a thick heavy bookboard, they are glued to the trimmed book blocks. They are then put into a book press, which helps to form the spine, and this completes the process.

D. For saddle-stitched books, the insides and covers are fed through a stitcher, folder, trimmer that puts two wire stitches (staples) in the center of the sheet at the fold, folds them in half, then trims the face to give you a smooth finished look.

Regardless of binding type, the books are then taken back to shipping, where they are shrinkwrapped in small groups (typically 5 books per pack, but thicker books will be less per pack, while thinner books will be more). They're placed very carefully into corrugated boxes—with packing added as needed—and the boxes are sealed shut with reinforced tape. (All of our packaging materials meet or exceed UPS's recommendations). The boxes are then labeled and put on a pallet, waiting for UPS to come and pick them up.

You'll be able to see your tracking number on your Order Details page, and track your packages on UPS.com.

A Word About Turn-Around Times

Keep in mind: we don't count Saturdays, Sundays or Holidays, and each day's cut-off is 5:00pm EST for Standard orders, 3:00pm EST for Rush orders, and Noon EST for SuperRush orders. So for standard orders, any approvals after 5:00pm EST will be counted as the following day. Also, hard cover (case bound) and spiral coil bound books take 5 business days to complete, so if you're ordering hard cover or coil bound books, use the second chart on page 95.

Example: If you OK your proof Monday at 4:45pm EST, your books will ship Wednesday. But if you wait 20 minutes longer and don't OK your proof until 5:05pm EST on Monday, the approval will be counted as Tuesday, so your books will ship Thursday.

Example of perfect bound order shipping to Florida:

SUN	MON	TUES	WED	THUR	FRI	SAT
					PLACE ORDER 5	CLOSED 6
	1	2	3	4		
CLOSED 7	APPROVE PROOF BY 5PM 8	PRINT DAY 1 9	PRINT DAY 2: BOOKS SHIP 10	IN TRANSIT VIA UPS 11	IN TRANSIT VIA UPS 12	CLOSED 13
CLOSED 14	BOOKS ARRIVE! 15	16	17	18	19	CLOSED 20

Got a "need-by" date? Let us know!

Your customer service rep will confirm your order
is on track every step of the way.

Book Production Schedule:

Perfect Bound books and Saddle-Stitched booklets

Proof OK'ed	Standard	Rush	SuperRush
the cut-off on this day ...	(cut-off is 5pm EST) Books will Ship ...	(cut-off is 3pm EST) Books will Ship	(cut-off is Noon EST,) Books will Ship ...
Monday	Wednesday	Tuesday*	Monday*
Tuesday	Thursday	Wednesday*	Tuesday*
Wednesday	Friday	Thursday*	Wednesday*
Thursday	Monday	Friday*	Thursday*
Friday	Tuesday	Monday*	Friday*
Saturday, Sunday	Wednesday	Tuesday*	Monday*

Hard Cover books and Coil-Bound books

Proof OK'ed	Standard	Rush	SuperRush
the cut-off on this day ...	(cut-off is 5pm EST) Books will Ship ...	(cut-off is 3pm EST) Books will Ship	(cut-off is Noon EST,) Books will Ship ...
Monday	Next Monday	Friday*	Thursday*
Tuesday	Next Tuesday	Monday*	Friday*
Wednesday	Next Wednesday	Tuesday*	Monday*
Thursday	Next Thursday	Wednesday*	Tuesday*
Friday	Next Friday	Thursday*	Wednesday*
Saturday, Sunday	Next Monday	Friday*	Thursday*

* Please CALL US for Rush or SuperRush. They are only available on a limited basis. Also, you'll need to give us enough time to get a PDF Proof back to you so that you can approve it by 3pm EST for Rushes, and by noon EST for SuperRushes.

You'll still need to add SHIPPING TIME. See the map on the next page for UPS Ground shipping time. Expedited shipping (Next Day Air, 2nd Day Air) is also available.

Using the table above and the map on the next page, you should be able to calculate exactly what day you'll receive your books. If you're not sure, just call us. We can help find the most inexpensive option for you to get books when you need them.

If you need to expedite either the printing and binding of your book or use urgent delivery (Next Day Air, 2nd Day Air, etc.), call us or email us IMMEDIATELY and request a change. We'll let you know if it can be done. Also, don't forget that spiral coil binding and hard cover (case bound books) take 1 week to produce.

Our standard shipping method is UPS Ground from Akron, Ohio or Las Vegas, Nevada. This map shows travel times from 48 Hour Books to anywhere in the U.S.A.

For example: 2 days to New York, 3 days to Florida.

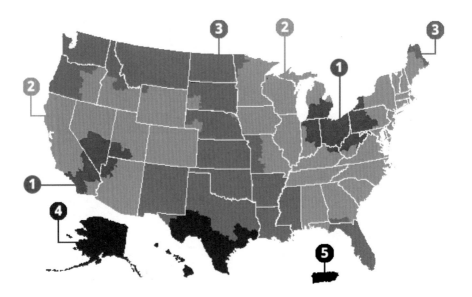

The day your books are delivered represents the culmination of weeks, months, even years of hard work on your part. Go ahead and celebrate. You've earned it! We've heard stories of people doing a dance, jumping up and down in excitement ... we've even had a couple authors hugging their UPS guy! So, pop the champagne ... your words are immortalized in print!

When you get a little free time, we'd appreciate it if you could drop us a note (email is fine) and tell us how you like your books. We always love hearing from our authors.

12

chapter twelve

Frequently Asked Questions

"The only stupid question is the question that is never asked."

—Ramon Bautista

Before we begin listing our FAQs, I wanted to mention three most commonly misunderstood items that probably cover 90% of the things that can go wrong with an order. If you keep these three items in mind as you go through the process, your order should travel smoothly (and inexpensively) through our shop.

Three Commonly Misunderstood Items ...

We understand that many of our authors are new to the publishing business. We do our best to offer help along the way, but sometimes they misunderstand how the process works. The best way to avoid possible errors is to educate our clients whenever possible. Whether you choose us or another book printer, do yourself a big favor and learn the three things that are commonly misunderstood. There are hundreds of things that can go wrong with a custom book printing order, but these three items probably cover 90% of them.

1. **We print your books according to your instructions, using your files.**

   - We give you a proof in order for you to catch any errors. It is your responsibility to carefully check every aspect of your proof. When you approve that proof, you take all responsibility for any errors in it.

2. **Never GUESS or ASSUME anything regarding your book order.**

   - Don't trust your computer screen for color matching. If getting the right colors is important to you, you MUST get a printed proof.
   - If you have questions about your order or your proof, ask us. We're happy to offer help. We want you to be happy with your books.
   - Sometimes, UPS misses a delivery date. Try to give yourself at least a one-day cushion on delivery.

3. **Our PrePress rules are critical to meeting your deadlines.**

   - We do a lot of work on your files before they are 'ready-to-print,' and this takes time. Every file is different ... they can take anywhere from an hour or two to a couple of days. We won't know how long your files will take until we've had a chance to examine them.
   - We have specific deadlines, and you must adhere to them if you need your books on a specific date. If your approval deadline is missed, you may have options to upgrade shipping, or to upgrade production (to "Rush" or "Super Rush"), or both.
   - There are additional costs for sending revised files or for having us make changes to your files.

Questions & Answers

Q. What if my book is an odd size?

A. Select the next larger size from our list of book sizes, then write the ACTUAL book size in the COMMENTS section of the order form. For example, a 5 x 7 book would be priced like a 5.5 x 8.5 book, and a 7 x 10 book would be priced like an 8.5 x 11 book.

Q. What does spiral Coil Binding cost?

A. We've simplified our charges for spiral coil binding. Compared to our regular perfect bound prices, black or white coil are 60¢ more per book, and specialty coil colors are 80¢ more per book.

It also takes a little longer to coil bind, so they're a 5-day standard turnaround. (Specialty coil colors may increase production time by up to 4 business days).

Unfortunately, if your book is over 350 pages, it's too thick to be spiral bound.

Q. What do Hard Covers cost?

A. Compared to our regular perfect bound prices, hard cover books are typically $10 more per book, but we do offer a special of converting 25 to hard cover for $210, which will save $40.

Q. Do you have book templates that I can use?

A. Yes, we do. You can download templates for free from our Templates Page (www.48HrBooks.com/free-book-templates). We currently have templates for Microsoft Word, which can be used in virtually any word processing program. They've been tested in Word, Word Perfect, Pages, and Open Office.

Q. How do I create a PDF file?

A. *(This is only if you've formatted your inside pages exactly the way that you want them. If you want us to do the reformatting for you, send us your Word document or other word processing file).*

1. Make sure your page size and margins are correct.

2. The two most important settings to check:
   - Be sure to embed all of your fonts
   - Do not downsample your graphics

3. Most word processing programs will let you select "File > Save as PDF" or "File > Print > Save as PDF," or "File > Export to PDF." If yours doesn't, there's still a Plan B. The following are instructions for creating a PDF from either Macintosh or Windows.

   On a Macintosh, you've already got everything you need. In virtually any program on a Mac, simply open your file and select 'Print.' A Print window will open. Be sure that you've selected the proper Page Size under Page Setup, then look at the bottom left corner and you'll find a drop-down labeled "PDF." Click on that, and choose "Save as PDF."

In Windows, download and install a program called "doPDF" from our website. You'll find the download link on our "Free Book Templates" page (www.48hrbooks.com/free-book-templates). It will install a virtual printer on your computer. Simply select it as your printer, and when you hit 'print', it will create a PDF file for you. It gives you an option of where to save it on your computer, so pay attention to where the PDF file gets saved. You'll also be able to use this virtual printer to convert other files on your computer to PDF.

Do the same with the file for your cover, and any other files you'll be sending us, then upload them all through our website. Simply log on with your email address and password, click the "Details" link to your order, and hit the "Add Files" button. Then drag your newly-created files onto the "Upload Files" box and hit "Upload."

Q. My PDF file is low-resolution. How do I fix that?

A. This may be caused by the settings you used when creating your PDF file, or it may be that the original graphics you're using are already low-resolution to begin with. Check your settings when you generate the PDF. Make sure they are not downsampling your graphics. If they give you a choice of resolution, choose 600 dpi.

If the artwork that you're using is already low-resolution to begin with, the only good way to fix that is to find better artwork. If they're scans that you made, you should rescan them at a higher resolution. For photographs, regardless of whether they're black-and-white or color, scan at 300 dpi. For line art, scan at 600 dpi. Then replace them in your document and try creating the PDF again.

Q. What is a bleed?

A. If you want your cover artwork to extend all the way to the edge of the cover (so it 'bleeds' off the cover), you'll need to extend that artwork BEYOND the edge of the cover at least 1/8". Some programs will create a bleed for you, but if you're not sure how to do it, simply create a page size that is 1/4" wider (1/8" added to the right, and 1/8" added to the left), and 1/4" taller (1/8" added to the top, and 1/8" added to the bottom), and make sure you keep any TYPE at least 3/8" away from the edges.

Q. What are your payment terms?

A. We accept Paypal, as well as the four major credit cards (Visa, Master Card, American Express and Discover), checks or wire transfers. Make check or money order payable to 48 Hour Books, and send to:

48 Hour Books
2249 14th St. SW
Akron, OH 44314

We don't require payment in full to get started, just a small deposit. We'll start working on your order, and send you a proof. Once you approve it, we require payment in full before we start printing your full order, so mailing a check may delay your order a little bit.

Q. What size do I make the cover?

A. Keep it simple. The easiest way to layout your cover is to do the front cover on one page (same size as the inside pages) and the back cover on a second page (same size as the inside pages). Don't have your type too close to the edge of the page or it may look bad after it's been trimmed down. And if you're going to have a bleed (where the artwork goes all the way to the edge of the cover), you'll want to add 1/8" to all sides.

If you want to, you can include the spine as a third page, but it should be a single line of type (title, author's name) that is as wide as the height of the book. Again, don't have your type too close to the edge of the page.

If you would rather send us the whole cover as one file, since it's a wrap-around cover, it needs to be TWICE the width of the finished book, plus the spine. To determine the width of your spine, divide number of pages (not SHEETS, but PAGES) by 440. For example, if your book was 120 pages, the spine would be 120 / 440 = 0.27 inches.

So for a 5.5 x 8.5 book that is 120 pages long, the cover should be 8.5 tall, and 11.27 wide (5.5 front + 5.5 back + .27 spine = 11.27).

And for an 8.5 x 11 book that is 200 pages long, the cover should be 11 tall, and 17.45 wide (8.5 front + 8.5 back + .45 spine = 17.45).

Include your title and author name on the spine so when your book is on a bookshelf, the title and author name read from top to bottom.

Q. Do you offer ISBN Numbers & barcodes?

A. Yes, we do. If you're planning on selling your books in stores, you'll need an ISBN. If your book doesn't have an ISBN, bookstores (including online bookstores) won't carry it.

Bookstores and book distributors use an ISBN to be sure they're ordering the correct book.

Each version of the book (paperback, hard cover, ePub, MOBI, PDF, audiobook, etc.) has it's own unique ISBN. So you might need 4 or 5 ISBNs just for one of your titles. That's why it may be smartest to order your ISBNs in blocks of 10, 100, or even 1,000. Keep in mind that once these numbers are assigned, they cannot be re-used.

Our ISBN packages include a free barcode for each ISBN. We'll set up your account with BooksInPrint.com, where all bookstores and book distributors go to find your book, and we'll provide you with detailed instructions for updating your book listings at BooksInPrint.com.

We receive ISBNs the day after they are ordered, so in some cases, it may add a day to your order.

Q. Can you print photos? Is there an extra charge?

A. Yes, we can print photos, and no, there is no extra charge for that. Black-and-white photos on the inside pages, and full-color photos on the cover are FREE. If you want full-color photos on the inside, just indicate how many pages of full-color you'd like when you fill out our SpecSheet.

Your book is printed digitally, so black-and-white photos on the inside pages will be printed as halftones. Full-color photos are printed as continuous tones, and are near photographic quality.

Q. Are my files OK?

A. You've probably spent many months, even years, writing your book. We HIGHLY recommend that you spend an extra hour or two looking it over one last time before you send it to us. It's best to make any last-minute corrections before you send us an imperfect file, in order to avoid any additional costs.

After you receive a proof, if you find corrections that have to be made, you might want to give us a call to discuss the most efficient (and least costly) way to get those corrections made. If you only have a few corrections, it's usually cheapest for US to make the changes on our system (we charge a very reasonable $75 per hour, so your changes may only cost a few dollars). But if you have a lot of changes, you may want to make the changes yourself and send us a new file. You can send revised files for a $50 fee, and if we have to re-format the new file, there may be an added cost for that, too. But call us first, and we can work out the best way to handle it.

Q. Do you want the PDF file in single page format, or in "spreads"?

A. Please, do NOT send us 'spreads.' Create a single PDF file with the entire inside portion of your book, but make sure the pages in your PDF are single pages, not spreads. Many programs will give you the option of printing in "spreads," which puts two pages together face-to-face on a single sheet. Our equipment is NOT designed for spreads, so please disable that feature before you create your PDFs. If your PDF files are in spreads, it will only delay the proof process.

Q. Need help with your files?

A. Is your page the wrong size? Some people have their book formatted for an 8.5 x 11 page, but they want the book to be 5.5 x 8.5, and they have no idea how to change their files. We can re-format your files for you. For basic re-formatting, we charge $125. If you have photos, charts, graphics or lots of chapter breaks, it may be a little higher: in that case, just send us the file and we'll look it over for free and give you a definite price.

Can't create a PDF? Our prices assume that you send us PDF files that are ready-to-print, but not everybody can do that. Some of our clients send us Microsoft Word documents, and we convert their files to PDF ($50 flat fee).

Q. What Types of Binding do you have available?

A. We offer four different binding styles.

PERFECT BINDING IS OUR STANDARD ...
...which are regular paperback books. This option is best if you have at least 16 pages.

We also offer case binding (hard cover books), plastic coil binding, and saddle stitching. Descriptions of each are below. This is the first decision you'll make when placing an order. Additional costs are shown on each choice to help you decide which is best for your book.

HARD COVER (CASE BINDING)
(recommended minimum of 40 pages)

We'll print your book with a full-color laminated hard cover. This process adds 3 days to your order, and about $10 per book to the cost. We can also split up your order, making some perfect bound and some hard cover. If you'd like that, first select perfect bound when placing your order. One of the last options is to convert 25 to hard cover. Select that and we'll make 25 of your books hard cover at a reduced rate of $210 ($8.40 additional per book, rather than the usual $10 additional per book).

SPIRAL COIL BINDING ...
(recommended up to 350 pages. If you have more than 350 pages, additional fees may apply)

Ideal for cookbooks or workbooks, anything that needs to be opened flat. It adds three days to your order and costs an extra 60¢ per book.

SADDLE-STITCHING ...
(only for booklets with less than 36 inside pgs) ...

We use two wire stitches (or staples) on the fold of booklets. It's the least expensive type of binding, but only for booklets with 36 inside pages or less. Because the pages are folded, saddle-stitched books must have a number of pages that is a multiple of four (4, 8, 16, 20, 24, 28, 32, or 36).

Q. What is your return policy or guarantee?

A. Since all of our books are custom printed, we do not accept returns unless there are manufacturing defects or damages in shipping. On the rare occasion that there is a defect in the manufacturing process or damage in shipping, please call or email us immediately and let us know what's wrong. We'll reprint the affected books and send them out to you at no additional charge. All claims of defects in manufacturing or damages in shipping must be made no later than 30 calendar days after delivery.

Q. Do you print index tabs?

A. Yes, we can print index tabs in your books. These are only available for spiral bound books. Pricing is available on the order form, so when you're placing an order, you'll see the extra cost. If you have questions, just call or email us. We'll be happy to help.

Q. Can You Help Me with Page Layout in Microsoft Word?

A. Read through Chapter 7 - Writing and Editing Your Book. It breaks things down in detail, but the bottom line is that you want to set up your pages and formatting the right way to save time and money.

SOME BASIC 'RULES-OF-THUMB':
- odd numbered pages should always be on the right.
- title page should be the first page (right hand page)
- copyright page should be the second page (left hand page)
- dedication, foreword, introduction, etc. should all be on right hand pages (odd numbers)
- chapters should all start on a right hand page (odd numbers)

Q. Do You Offer Cream colored paper?

A. Yes, we do. Near the end of this book we have sample pages that are printed on our 60# Cream offset. When you place your order, you'll be able to select what paper you want, and each paper type shows the additional cost. So if you'd like a softer look for your books, just select "Cream Paper" on our order form.

Q. How hard is filling out the order form?

A. It's so easy. Fill out information about your book, about yourself, and your shipping and payment information. If you have questions, just click the 'More Info' button, and you'll see answers to your questions. Or, give us a call, and we'll be happy to walk you through the whole process.

SOME COMMON MISTAKES:

'PAGES' VS. 'SHEETS'

You should always figure your book in terms of 'pages' and not 'sheets'. You wouldn't say that a Stephen King novel is '330 sheets' long, you'd say it's '660 pages' long. There are two pages on each sheet of paper, so be sure to enter the number of 'pages' in your book, or your price won't be accurate.

'# OF FULL-COLOR PAGES'

Only enter the number of INSIDE pages that will be printed in full-color. Don't include the covers, since we print them in full color for free.

COVER DESIGN

If you need help with your cover design, our Create-a-Cover option may be perfect for you. Simply choose one of our cover templates, select two colors, and send us any photography, artwork, and text that you want included. Be sure to send wording and artwork for the back cover, too. It's included in the cost.

TYPE OF BINDING

Our standard type of binding is "perfect binding," like a paperback book. We also offer spiral coil binding (which adds

60¢ per book), hard cover (case bound - which adds $10 per book) and saddle-stitching (two staples on the center fold - same price as perfect bound).

Q. Is your coil made of plastic or metal?

A. We use a heavy gauge plastic coil, which is the industry standard. While there is some metal coil out there (like Wire-O binding), it's very thin, and is easily bent or kinked. Our plastic coil is much more forgiving.

Q. What kind of proofs will I get?

A. On all new orders, you'll always receive a PDF Proof to approve. After you've approved that, we can send you a Printed Proof: one complete book, printed and bound like your full order will be. It's really the only fool-proof way to check color matching. And many people catch file errors better when viewing an actual book. If there's a mistake in your files, wouldn't it be better to catch it on your Printed Proof, rather than after your entire order is printed?

We highly recommend getting a Printed Proof, especially for first-time authors. It can save you a lot of money. Getting a Printed Proof can save you hundreds, even thousands, of dollars.

If you would like a Printed Proof in addition to your PDF Proof, say "Yes" to Printed Proof when you place your order. After you've approved your PDF Proof, we will print, bind and ship one complete book for you. The printed proof costs $40.

Of course, on future reprint orders, if it's an Exact Reprint (meaning there are no artwork or text changes), you won't get a PDF Proof. Since we'll be using the existing files, your job will go straight into print.

Q. What if I have special instructions?

A. If you have any special instructions (special book size or shipping instructions, etc.), PLEASE include them in the comments section. This way, your special instructions won't be missed by our workers when they're filling your order.

Still Have Questions?

If you still have questions about any aspect of your order, from layout to shipping, we're here to help you. Simply call, email or on-line chat. We'll get you the answers you need as quickly as possible.

Toll-Free Nationwide: 800-231-0521

Outside the U.S.:	1-330-374-6917
email:	info@48HrBooks.com
Or chat online at:	www.48HrBooks.com

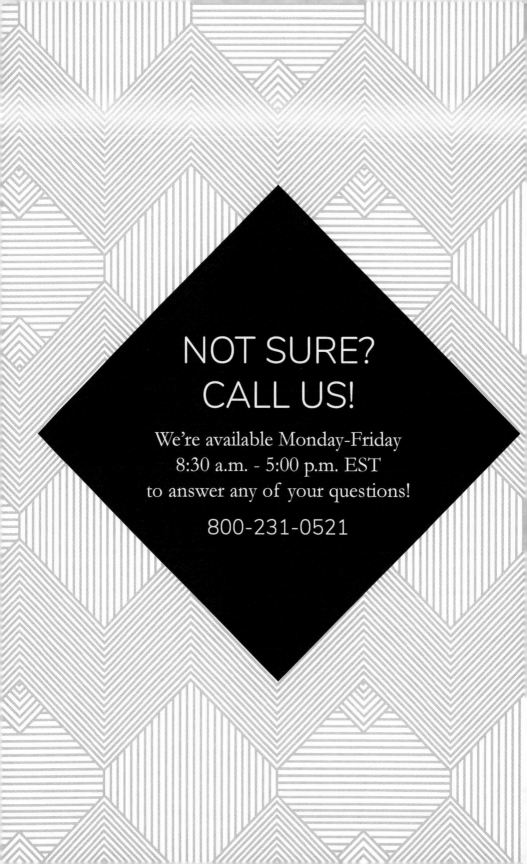

NOT SURE?
CALL US!

We're available Monday-Friday
8:30 a.m. - 5:00 p.m. EST
to answer any of your questions!

800-231-0521

13

chapter thirteen

Terms & Conditions of Sale

SAMPLE: Navy Leatherette
with silver Diamond 3D Foil

Please pay special attention to the bold areas:
items 8 thru 10 and 19.

We cannot stress this enough: When a customer approves a proof, if there are mistakes in that proof, even if there are mistakes that the printer made, those mistakes are not the responsibility of the printer. We give you a proof in order to check all work—yours and ours. So please, look over your proof carefully. We cannot reprint any orders if mistakes in the finished books were also in the proof. This policy is not unique to 48 Hour Books, it is universally accepted by printers everywhere.

We want you to be happy with your books, so please take the time to look over your proof thoroughly before approving it. No matter how many times you've proofread, it's best to give your book one final look before it's too late to make changes.

1. Quotations/Estimates ~ A quotation not accepted within 30 days may be changed.

2. Orders ~ Acceptance of orders is subject to contingencies such as fire, water, strikes, theft, vandalism, act of God, and other causes beyond 48 Hr Books's control. Canceled orders require compensation for incurred costs and related obligations.

3. Experimental Work ~ Experimental or preliminary work performed at the customer's request will be charged to the customer at 48 Hr Books's current rates. This work may not be used without 48 Hr Books's written consent.

4. Creative Work ~ Sketches, copy, dummies, and all other creative work developed or furnished by 48 Hr Books are 48 Hr Books's exclusive property. 48 Hr Books must give written approval for all use of this work and for any derivation of ideas from it.

5. Accuracy of Specifications ~ Quotations are based on the accuracy of the specifications provided. 48 Hr Books can requote a job at the time of submission if copy, artwork, or other materials do not conform to the information on which the original quotation was based.

6. Venue ~ In the event of suit regarding this contract, the venue and jurisdiction therefore shall be in either the Superior or Municipal Court, as appropriate, of the county of Summit, Ohio. The parties agree and stipulate that the essential terms of this contract are to be performed in said County.

7. Electronic Manuscripts/Images ~ It is the customer's responsibility to maintain a copy of the original file. 48 Hr Books is not responsible for accidental damage to media supplied by the customer or for the accuracy of furnished input or final output. Until digital input can be evaluated by 48 Hr Books, no claims or promises are made about 48 Hr Books's ability to work with jobs submitted in digital format, and no liability is assumed for problems that may

arise. Any additional translating, editing, or programming needed to utilize customer-supplied files will be charged at prevailing rates.

8. **Alterations/Corrections ~ Customer alterations include all work performed in addition to the original specifications. All such work will be charged at 48 Hr Books's current rates.**

9. **PDF Proofs and Printed Proofs ~ 48 Hr Books will submit PDF proofs (soft proofs) for the customer's review and approval. Upon request, 48 Hr Books can also provide a Printed Proof after the PDF Proof has been approved. In both cases, the customer should examine the proofs carefully, and respond with either "Approved -- O.K. to print as is" or "Rejected -- corrections required." All corrections must be submitted in writing, and sent in a single email to 48 Hr Books. Multiple emails will delay your order, and may incur additional costs.**

10. **Undetected errors ~ 48 Hr Books will not be responsible for undetected production errors if:**

    •   **Proofs are not required by the customer, or**
    •   **The work is printed per the customer's OK, or**
    •   **Requests for changes are communicated verbally.**

11. Color Proofing ~ If you have critical color-matching requirements on your order, 48 Hr Books highly recommends that you request a Printed Proof. Because of differences in the way monitors display color and the way printing presses print color, a variation in color between the customer's monitor and the completed job is to be expected. When a color variation of this kind occurs, it will be considered acceptable performance.

12. Overruns/Underruns ~ Overruns or underruns will not exceed 10 percent of the quantity ordered. 48 Hr Books will bill for the actual quantity delivered within this tolerance. If the customer re-

quires a guaranteed quantity, the percentage of tolerance must be stated at the time of quotation.

13. Customer's Property ~ 48 Hr Books will only maintain fire and extended coverage on property belonging to the customer while the property is in 48 Hr Books's possession. 48 Hr Books's liability for such property will not exceed the amount recoverable from the insurance. Additional insurance coverage may be obtained if it is requested in writing and if the premium is paid to 48 Hr Books.

14. Delivery ~ Unless otherwise specified, the price quoted is for a single shipment, without storage, F.O.B. 48 Hr Books's platform. Proposals are based on continuous and uninterrupted delivery of the complete order. If the specifications state otherwise, 48 Hr Books will charge accordingly at current rates. Charges for delivery of materials and supplies from the customer to 48 Hr Books or from the customer's supplier to 48 Hr Books are not included in quotations unless specified. Title for finished work passes to the customer upon delivery to the carrier at the shipping point or upon mailing of invoices for the finished work or a portion thereof, whichever occurs first.

15. Production Schedules ~ Production schedules will be established and followed by both the customer and 48 Hr Books. There will be no liability or penalty for delays due to a state of war, riot, civil disorder, fire, strikes, accidents, action of government or civil authority, acts of God, or other cases beyond the control of 48 Hr Books. In such cases, schedules will be extended by an amount of time equal to the delay incurred.

16. Customer-Furnished Materials ~ Materials furnished by customers or their suppliers are verified by delivery tickets. 48 Hr Books bears no responsibility for discrepancies between delivery tickets and actual counts. Customer supplied paper must be delivered according to specifications furnished by 48 Hr Books. These specifications will include correct weight, thickness, pick resistance, and other

technical requirements. Artwork, film, color separations, special dies, tapes, disks, or other materials furnished by the customer must be usable by 48 Hr Books without alteration or repair. Items not meeting this requirement will be repaired by the customer or by 48 Hr Books at 48 Hr Books's current rates.

17. Outside Purchases ~ Unless otherwise agreed in writing, all outside purchases as requested or authorized by the customer, are chargeable.

18. Payment Terms ~ Payment is net cash, and must be paid in full before we begin production of your full order. We accept Visa, Master Card, Discover and American Express, as well as Paypal. Regular checks (including Paypal's eChecks) and money orders can also be sent, but this may delay your order. All unpaid invoices are subject to a finance charge of 2% per month.

19. **Claims for defects ~ Claims for defects, damages, or shortages must be made by the customer in writing no later than 30 calendar days after delivery. If no such claim is made, 48 Hr Books and the customer will understand that the job has been accepted. By accepting the job, the customer acknowledges that 48 Hr Books's performance has fully satisfied all terms, conditions, and specifications. 48 Hr Books's Liability will be limited to the quoted printing and binding price of defective goods without additional charge for special or consequential damages. As security for payment of any sum due under the terms of an agreement, 48 Hr Books has the right to hold and place a lien on all customer property in 48 Hr Books's possession. This right applies even if credit has been extended, notes have been accepted, trade acceptances have been made, or payment has been guaranteed. If payment is not made, the customer is liable for all collection costs incurred.**

20. Liability ~ Disclaimer of Express Warranties ~ 48 Hr Books warrants that the work is as described in the purchase order. The customer understands that all sketches, copy, dummies, and preparatory work shown to the customer are intended only to illustrate the general type and quality of the work. They are not intended to represent the actual work performed.

   ~ Disclaimer of Implied Warranties ~ 48 Hr Books warrants only that the work will conform to the description contained in the purchase order. 48 Hr Books's maximum liability, whether by negligence, contract, or otherwise, will not exceed the return of the amount invoiced for the work in the dispute. Under no circumstances will 48 Hr Books be liable for specific, individual, or consequential damages.

21. Indemnification ~ The customer agrees to protect 48 Hr Books from economic loss and any other harmful consequences that might arise in connection with the work. This means the customer will hold 48 Hr Books harmless and save, indemnify, and otherwise defend 48 Hr Books against claims, demands, actions, and proceedings on any and all grounds. This will apply regardless of responsibility for negligence.

22. Copyrights ~ The customer also warrants that the subject matter to be printed is not copyrighted by a third party. The customer also recognizes that because subject matter does not have to bear a copyright notice to be protected by copyright law, absence of such notice does not necessarily assure a right to reproduce. The customer further warrants that no copyright notice has been removed from any material used in preparing the subject matter for reproduction. To support these warranties, the customer agrees to indemnify and hold 48 Hr Books harmless for all liability, damages, and attorney fees that may be incurred in any legal action connected with copyright infringement involving the work produced or provided.

23. Personal or Economic Rights ~ The customer also warrants that the work does not contain anything that is libelous or scandalous or anything that threatens anyone's right to privacy or other personal or economic rights. The customer will, at the customer's sole expense, promptly and thoroughly defend 48 Hr Books in all legal actions on these grounds as long as 48 Hr Books promptly notifies the customer of legal action, and gives the customer reasonable time to undertake and conduct a defense. 48 Hr Books reserves the right to use its sole discretion in refusing to print anything 48 Hr Books deems libelous, scandalous, improper, or infringing on copyright law.

24. Storage ~ 48 Hr Books retains copies of production files used until the related end product has been accepted by the customer. If requested by the customer, intermediate materials will be stored for an additional period at an additional charge. 48 Hr Books is not liable for any loss or damage to stored material beyond what is recoverable by 48 Hr Books's fire and extended insurance coverage.

25. Taxes ~ All taxes and assessments levied by any governmental authority are the responsibility of the customer. All amounts due for taxes and assessments will be added to the customer's invoice. If, after the customer has paid the invoice, it is determined that more tax is due, then the customer must promptly remit the required taxes to 48 Hr Books for any additional taxes paid.

26. Telecommunications ~ 48 Hr Books is not responsible for any errors, omissions, or extra costs resulting from faults in transmission.

27. Preparatory Material -- Any intermittent computer files that we create in order to print your books shall remain 48 Hr Books's property. However, this does not include the actual words and images of your book. Those words and images remain as your exclusive property, and 48 Hr Books claims no rights to them.

PRINTING TRADE CUSTOMS

What are Trade Customs?

In the technical language of the Uniform Commercial Code, a trade custom is defined as: "any practice or method of dealing having such regularity of observation in a place, vocation or trade as to justify an expectation that it will be observed with respect to the transaction in question."

The Trade Customs of the printing industry of North America were originally formally promulgated at the Annual Convention of the United Typothetae of America in 1922. They have been updated and repopulated five times since then - most recently in 2003 by Printing Industries of America, National Association of Printers and Lithographers and Graphic Arts Technical Foundation and renamed to "Suggested Terms & Conditions of Sale."

14

chapter fourteen

A Word About Paper and the Environment

Yes, we use recycled, acid-free paper. In addition, all of our paper is certified by either SFI (Sustainable Forestry Initiative) or FSC (Forest Stewardship Council), two independent groups that act as watchdogs for all commercial forestry. Since we use digital presses, we have very little waste paper, and what waste we do have is all recycled. Paper, by the way, is one of the most easily recycled materials on earth, as well as one of the most biodegradable when it's thrown out.

Everybody's seen the message at the bottom of some emails that says, "Consider the environment before printing this email." We respectfully disagree. In fact, we think a more appropriate message might be: "It's OK to print this email. Paper is one of the most biodegradable, renewable, and sustainable products on earth. Thanks to improved forest management, we have more trees today than we had 100 years ago. But that's only true because we need trees for wood and paper. The day we stop using wood and paper products, we'll stop needing forests."

Sure, trees are cut down to make paper, but the paper companies plant more trees than they cut, so they aren't contributing to deforestation. Quite the opposite ... they're maintaining the forests. It's in their best interest to keep the forests intact. In fact, if we were ever to truly become a paperless society, most of our forests would be cut down so the land could be used for other, more profitable business.

So if you really want to save the forests, you may want to print that email after all.

15

chapter fifteen

Paper Samples

Boon and Mary Delilah Francis; 1880 census, Linton IA

PAPER OPTIONS:

60# Bright White Offset (our standard book paper)

70# Bright White Offset

80# Bright White Offset

60# Cream Offset

70# Cream Offset

80# Silk Text

100# Silk Text

80# Gloss Text

100# Gloss Text

COVER OPTIONS:

Check out the included samples or ask us to send sample swatches of any of these covers

10 pt. C1S with Gloss UV *(featured on page 5)*

10 pt. C1S Silk Laminate *(featured on cover & page 23)*

10 pt. C1S Hi-Gloss Laminate *(featured on page 33)*

12 pt. C1S with Gloss UV *(featured on page 49)*

12 pt. C1S Silk Laminate

12 pt. C1S Hi-Gloss Laminate

80# Smooth Cover (with no coating) *(featured on page 63)*

80# Linen Cover (with no coating) *(featured on page 89)*

Leatherette (for all binding types) *(featured on page 115)*

Leather (for hard cover books only)

Pearl Linen Cloth (for hard cover books only)

GET A
FEEL FOR IT

Our <u>standard</u> paper is excellent quality—
and we offer several upgraded finishes, too!

Check out how photos print on our
different paper stocks (in color
or in black & white)

60# Bright White Offset (our standard book paper)
Printed on our color press

60# Bright White Offset (our standard book paper)
Printed in black & white on our color press

60# Bright White Offset (our standard book paper)
Printed on our black & white press

60# Bright White Offset (our standard book paper)

70# Bright White Offset
Printed in black & white on our color press

70# Bright White Offset
Printed on our black & white press

70# Bright White Offset

80# Bright White Offset
Printed on our color press

80# Bright White Offset
Printed in black & white on our color press

80# Bright White Offset
Printed on our black & white press

80# Bright White Offset

60# Cream Offset
Printed on our color press

60# Cream Offset
Printed in black & white on our color press

60# Cream Offset
Printed on our black & white press

60# Cream Offset

70# Cream Offset
Printed on our color press

70# Cream Offset
Printed in black & white on our color press

70# Cream Offset
Printed on our black & white press

70# Cream Offset

80# Silk Text
Printed in black & white on our color press

80# Silk Text

100# Silk Text
Printed in black & white on our color press

80# Gloss Text
Printed on our color press

80# Gloss Text
Printed in black & white on our color press

80# Gloss Text

100# Gloss Text
Printed in black & white on our color press